A Year of Grace

Exploring the Christian Seasons

David Hoyle

CANTERBURY
PRESS

Norwich

© David Hoyle 2019

First published in 2019 by the Canterbury Press Norwich
Editorial office
3rd Floor, Invicta House
108–114 Golden Lane
London EC1Y 0TG, UK

www.canterburypress.co.uk

Canterbury Press is an imprint of Hymns Ancient & Modern Ltd
(a registered charity)

Hymns Ancient & Modern® is a registered trademark of
Hymns Ancient & Modern Ltd
13A Hellesdon Park Road, Norwich,
Norfolk NR6 5DR, UK

Scripture quotations are from the New Revised Standard Version
of the Bible, copyright 1989 by the Division of Christian Education
of the National Council of the Churches of Christ in the USA.
Used by permission. All rights reserved.

British Library Cataloguing in Publication data

A catalogue record for this book is available
from the British Library

978-1-78622-033-2

Typeset by Manila Typesetting Company
Printed and bound in Great Britain by
CPI Group (UK) Ltd

For Katy.
With love.

How but in custom and in ceremony
Are innocence and beauty born?
W. B. Yeats

Contents

Preface

This book had its beginnings while I was on sabbatical leave and a guest in Peterhouse, in Cambridge. I am grateful to the Governing Body of the College for their generous hospitality and particularly thank the Master, Professor Adrian Dixon, for the welcome and kindness he extended throughout my stay. My colleagues in Bristol have (again) been very patient with me as I gave time to writing and the cathedral congregation kindly put up with me thinking aloud in some of my sermons. Without the help of Sarah Morris, who looks after my diary, I would never have crossed the finishing line. Stephen Hampton read the text and saved me from error. I hope he was compensated, a little, by the enjoyment he had in pointing the error out. Particular thanks go to Tom Clammer, sometime Precentor of Salisbury, who brought the eye of a liturgist and scholar to the text. His insights were invaluable, and some of them are incorporated in the text. Mistakes that remain are all my own.

Christine Smith at the Canterbury Press has been a model of patience and a constant encouragement. Her colleagues have been a delight to work with.

Janet graciously continues to put up with my preoccupations and a particularly trying tendency to seek out, and then explain, ecclesiastical detail on each and every holiday. Mike kept me cheerful. This book, though, is dedicated to Katy, who wondered if it would ever be finished.

The truth is, there is still some way to go.

David Hoyle
December 2018

O Oriens, splendor lucis aeternae, et sol iustitiae:
veni, et illumina sedentes in tenebris et umbra mortis.

O dawn of the east, brightness of light eternal, and sun of justice:
come, and enlighten those who sit in darkness and in the shadow of death.

Do This

As a boy, I stayed occasionally with my grandparents, in their quiet and ordered house near the Fylde coast, in Lancashire. They were kind, but not at all sure what to do with me. There were long hours when I entertained myself, discovering that nearly all the books were large, and serious, and short of pictures. There was however, curiously, a bound collection of *Punch*, 20 volumes, published in the 1920s. Each volume had a theme. Nearly 100 years on, they sound very dated: *Mr Punch in London Town, Mr Punch Goes Motoring*. I can name check the titles because these books sit on my shelves now, and they can still transport me back to Wrea Green, more than 50 years ago. It was there that I found a cartoon of a well-dressed woman struggling to find the correct collect and readings in her *Book of Common Prayer*. 'Which Sunday is it?' she whispers, as the service begins. Her husband looks like a man who devoutly wishes he were somewhere else. Distracted, he replies, 'The Second Sunday after Ascot.'

Only later, when I started going to church myself, could I make any sense of this cartoon. I grew up knowing nothing about Epiphany, the Sunday next before Easter, or the Sundays after Trinity. When I started putting that right, I joined a generation of Anglicans who had problems that *Punch* never knew, as I juggled one new service book after another. I worked my way through *Series Two, Series Three*, and *The Alternative Service Book*, watching the books get bigger, as my choices grew. By 1980, I had acquired a calendar of readings that demanded that I know not just which Sunday it was, but whether it was *Year One* or *Year Two*. Now, I navigate *Common Worship* and

I have a whole library of texts to use. I have to pause now and again, and remind myself that at 10 a.m. this morning we will use the readings for the Fourth Sunday of Epiphany, but at 8 a.m. another congregation will be told that this is the Third Sunday after Epiphany.

Years into this liturgical revision, I heard Robert Runcie lament over an unintended consequence of all this change. He was well aware that new forms of worship gave us good things to enjoy, but he was still sorry that he no longer knew the Eucharistic Prayer by heart. Sunday by Sunday, the texts varied and now he had to read it more than he could pray it. More recently, Michael Perham, then Bishop of Gloucester, told a clergy conference that we had become weighed down with all our new texts (some of which he had written). A priest stands at an altar and greets the congregation with the words, 'The Lord be with you'. It is a good beginning; the trouble is, no one looks up. Everyone is staring at the book, or at a distant screen, straining for the next cue. We are, more than ever, *people of the book*, but the book is no longer the Bible, it is the liturgy, a pamphlet handed out at the door, or perhaps even an image thrown up on a screen.

Now, I work in a cathedral where we are ever eager to make this year even more interesting and memorable than last. We thumb the pages of *Common Worship* and devise ever better ways of observing Advent, Epiphany and Easter. So, just in case you come to doubt it, I will set down here my gratitude for all the riches that liturgical revision has given us; three cheers for *Common Worship*. Even so, like Robert Runcie, I am allowed to note and regret some unintended consequences. We have choices we did not have, but choices can be challenging and you have to know *this* from *that*. At the beginning of each and every day, at Morning Prayer, I encounter one of the awkward outcomes of all our options. As a parish priest, I quite often prayed alone. In cathedrals, you can reliably expect people to come to say Morning Prayer with you. Not just clergy colleagues, but a faithful little congregation tipping up day by day, and quite often a fair smattering of visitors. We should be pleased. We are pleased, but we are also back in the world of that *Punch* cartoon. To follow Morning Prayer, we need to know the day of the week, the season of the year, and ideally, also to be clear whether or not today happens to be a saint's day. It also helps not to be colour blind, as you skip from one blue, yellow or green, beribboned page, to another. To get through this service, you need a guide. So, we have produced one. Even so, the officiant still needs to issue the odd instruction. When I was first ordained (and we were all getting used to another new service book) I can remember a colleague standing at the altar and saying, 'As our Lord taught us, on page one hundred and fifty, we say together . . .' We try not to do that in the cathedral, but we still plunge, daily, into commentary and stage management. It is not just that we have to bury our eyes in the book that I mind; it is more the fact that prayer becomes such a fussy activity of turning pages and knowing the rules. Either it is something that only the initiated can manage, a closely guarded secret full of knowing glances and grimaces; or it is littered with instructions. Either way, what this kind of worship really demonstrates is the need to be *in the know*. We have made Morning Prayer something you have to master. We have turned it into a possession. Doing that, we have managed to get things precisely the wrong way round. On occasional trips to London I sometimes say Morning Prayer at the Royal Foundation of St Katharine in Limehouse. As I try to work out what it is we are doing I see a splendid text carved into the floor (a quotation from St Augustine): 'We do not come to God by navigation, but by love.' Quite.

Just a little too often we have turned Christian worship into an encounter with a book, the struggle to find our place. This book, this little study of the Christian year, is written because I believe we have only got that half right. We do indeed go to church to find our place. That is *exactly* what we do. To find our place, however, we should not have our eyes fixed anxiously on page numbers; we should be listening and looking for something altogether more interesting. Christian faith and Christian worship issue an invitation to find our place in history, and in God's future. It is not an activity we have to master, but something we have to surrender to. It really is all about knowing your place.

The cycle of the Christian year, Lent, Holy Week, Easter, Ascension, and the richness of the worship that goes with them, all tell a story and we are asked to join in. Morning Prayer may feel as though it is an exercise in literacy, but in truth it is part of a drama and we are members of the cast. It should have us looking up and looking about. Church is not a constraint and it should never be an extra commitment, a duty added on to daily life, like going to the gym. The worship of the Church is our direction of travel, our future, our purpose. To go to church is to come home. It is in that sense that we find our place in the liturgy. Whatever it is, it is certainly not something that we will ever *manage*, or *possess*. Done properly, the Christian year with its routines teaches us and changes us.

Long years after first looking at cartoons in *Punch*, I became a student preparing for ordination as deacon and priest. Like so many others, I came across a very famous passage about the Eucharist in one of the best-known books about Anglican liturgy. Writing before World War Two, in rather purple prose, the monk and scholar Dom Gregory Dix reflected on Christ's command to 'Do this in remembrance of me':

Was ever another command so obeyed? . . . Men have found no better thing than this to do for kings at their crowning and for criminals going to the scaffold; for armies in triumph or for a bride and bridegroom in a little country church; for the wisdom of the Parliament of a mighty nation or for a sick old woman afraid to die; for a schoolboy sitting an examination or for Columbus setting out to discover America; because the Turk was at the gates of Vienna; for the repentance of Margaret; while the lions roared in the nearby amphitheatre; on the beach at Dunkirk; while the hiss of scythes in the thick June grass came faintly through the windows of the church; tremulously, by an old monk on the fiftieth anniversary of his vows; furtively, by an exiled bishop who had hewn timber all day in a prison camp near Murmansk; gorgeously, for the canonisation of S. Joan of Arc – one could fill many pages with the reasons why men have done this, and not tell a hundredth part of them.[1]

Dix had that kind of confidence that the routines of worship can reach into any situation. He was expressing that confidence, but saying something more. It is not just that the liturgy is robust enough to serve on any occasion. Dix knew that the liturgy *does* something.

> And best of all, week by week and month by month, on a hundred thousand successive Sundays, faithfully, unfailingly, across all the parishes of Christendom, the pastors have done this just to make the plebs sancta Dei – the holy common people of God.[2]

The liturgy makes us into something we were not. It changes me, and I find it is not *me*, it is *us*. Our worship forms a community. Writing about a prayer routinely used in primers in the early sixteenth century (the *Salve Salutaris Hosti*), Eamon Duffy observes:

> At the climax of the prayer this new life is seen as essentially communal not individualistic. The communicant prays that *I may be worthy to be incorporated into your body which is the Church. May I be one of Your members, and may You be in my head . . .*[3]

Going to church for Christmas, or Easter, or going there Sunday by Sunday, we step into a story that is being told and we try to find our place. This book is an attempt to explain a little of the story that is being told in the hope that we might find our place a little more easily.

Here is the story that is told, year after year, in all those places where we meet 'in remembrance' of him. Here is the story that was (and is) about him, but is also about us. Just before you begin, I should explain that I think there is a texture to this story that we too often overlook. If this book does not seem to give you quite what you thought you had a right to expect, bear with me. There is something I want to say to you.

Notes

1 Dom Gregory Dix, *The Shape of the Liturgy* (Edinburgh: A&C Black, 1945), p. 744.

2 Dix, *Shape of the Liturgy*, p. 744.

3 E. Duffy, *The Stripping of the Altars: Traditional Religion in England, 1400–1580* (New Haven, CT: Yale University Press, 2005), p. 93.

Advent
Giving the future back to God

The beginning of the year and the end of everything

The city of Wells on a November evening that heralded winter.
It had turned colder, and was getting darker on the deserted
streets as two of us walked back to a car. A new dean had just
begun his ministry in the cathedral. In the gathering shadows
of the nave, his sermon was a promise of a bright future; it
was confident, stylish and compelling. Outside, in the dusk,
we talked about the new dean and that sermon. Then my companion paused and pointed to some flats just ahead of us. 'The
plan was,' he said, 'that when I got really old, we would move
here.' We stopped and looked in silence. I had nothing sensible
to say. My companion was Michael Perham, who had been my
bishop when I worked in Gloucester. He was a man who saw
possibilities, believed in the future and wanted us to get there
together. Now retired, he still felt very much like *my* bishop,
but he had become a friend, and here he was, talking about
dying. We both knew that he would never make the move into
those flats. We both knew that he would not live into old age.
So while a new dean planned for the future, seizing it by the
scruff of the neck, Michael was in the business of letting go.

On that November evening, Advent had not quite started, but
death, one of the great Advent themes, confronted us. It tugged
at our sleeves and demanded our attention. We needed the words
we might use, but even for a bishop and a priest accustomed to
facing up to mortality, the words did not come easily. We did

talk about death, but there were silences and I know I hesitated a little. Some things are very hard to describe and discuss. I think it is significant that the Christian year starts by posing some of these hardest of all questions, making us confront the limits of understanding and the breaking point of our vocabulary. Advent is the season of last things, it is the conversation we have been putting off. It is, and should be, a challenge. This season where we make a beginning does not duck difficulty.

Michael loved Advent. It teaches us, he said,

> that there may already be glory in our midst, but in the plan of God there is more glory still to come.[1]

Throughout his ministry, he tried to persuade the rest of us to make the most of Advent. He wrote books about the seasons. He had an overflowing, infectious enthusiasm for the right liturgy and the right mood for the time of year. That was not a merely liturgical interest; Michael loved the routines of the life of faith because they changed things. His last book, *The Way of Christ-Likeness*, had the subtitle *Being Transformed by the Liturgies of Lent, Holy Week and Easter*. At the end of that book he wrote:

> If I urge people and communities to have a deeper, richer and more fulfilling experience of the 40 days of Lent, of Holy Week and of the Great Fifty Days of Easter, it is only that they may have an opportunity to be transformed by the experience.[2]

He enjoyed the procession of liturgical seasons in much the same way that a keen walker might delight in a good map, because it shows you the *whole* journey and because you can trust it. It is fair to say, though, that even he found Advent a bit of a challenge.

Advent looks to Christmas, of course it does, but then it *keeps* looking; it looks far beyond. There are interesting conversations about how you can make use of Advent as a month of preparing to greet the Christ who comes to us at Christmas. There are prayers you can use; there are candles you can light. Doing that, you measure out a few weeks and add a bit of lustre and meaning to the preparations you make at home. It is quite another thing, though, to think about what it might mean for God to fulfil the prayer we keep praying and, finally and conclusively, for his kingdom to come. A conversation about *that* must gather up not just what we have to say about death but also take in judgement, heaven and hell. Small wonder Michael and I fell silent as we thought about death and dying and looked at the flat that he would never occupy.

Knowing and not knowing

Always honest about the difficulty and himself, Michael wrote:

> Like many Christians, I live with a dilemma. I cannot entirely make sense of the end-of-time language of the New Testament . . . Yet I am deeply unhappy with attempts to reinterpret such language out of existence.[3]

He was talking about the readings you might hear on Advent Sunday, or in the days that follow, readings that paint vivid and unsettling pictures:

> signs in the sun, the moon, and the stars, and on the earth distress among nations confused by the roaring of the sea and the waves. People will faint from fear and foreboding of what is coming upon the world. (Luke 21.25–26)

Passages like that (and there are plenty of them) are challenging for a number of reasons. There are questions about *when* this might happen that have prompted all sorts of cock-eyed speculation. There are questions about *why* this should happen: why would a good and creative God suddenly unleash such destruction? There are also questions about *whether* this will happen. This kind of writing always assumes that we are near the end, that *this* is the final stage of human history and soon there will be a shattering unveiling of God's great purposes. As the moment keeps getting deferred, we begin to wonder if this is not perhaps a kind of myth, a story told with purpose but not, perhaps, a precise description of this moment and the moment after. Starting the Christian year with readings like this, we can make a very uncertain beginning.

We need to get our bearings. The readings we hear at Advent come out of a particular tradition of writing. Luke, writing about signs in the sun and stars, sounds very like some of the prophets whose words had been written down long before. Joel, for example, speaks of

> portents in the heavens and on the earth, blood and fire and columns of smoke. The sun shall be turned to darkness, and the moon to blood. (Joel 2.30–11)

This is what biblical scholars call *apocalypse*, which is a word that means *uncovering*. One of the readings you might hear on Advent Sunday is pretty explicit: 'O that you would tear open the heavens and come down, so that the mountains would quake at your presence' (Isaiah 64.1). An apocalypse opens the heavens and shows us mysteries we did not know. This kind of passage is supposed to show us something, but what exactly is it that we are being shown?

I have already suggested that this kind of writing might sound a bit like myth. In fact, it is a rather particular kind of history. Admittedly, it does not sound like history. That is because the way we write history now is careful and scholarly. Historians write essays on hyperinflation in the Weimar Republic and show how that led to the rise of National Socialism (historians do not have much difficulty sleeping). One thing leads to another; there are causes, consequences and progress. Apocalypse, though, feels like a different thing altogether; cause and effect are nowhere to be seen, everything is out of proportion. It is as if you asked your aunt if she would prefer tea or coffee and in response she has set fire to your trousers. One thing does not lead to another.

In fact, the prophets who went in for this kind of language were writing out of a shattering and uncomfortable experience of history, invasion, defeat, destruction and exile. Their history was red in tooth and claw. They described the plight of a tiny nation crushed by superpowers. The language might sound extravagant, but then their experience was overwhelming. This was what it felt like; this was the way things were. This was a particular history.

In a recent row about 'Thought for the Day', on Radio 4's *Today* programme, Justin Webb suggested that the religious message amounts to nothing more than bland reassurance: 'If everyone was nicer to everyone else, it would be fine.' 'No,' say the prophets. 'That is not what we are saying.' The message of the prophets is that death and war and catastrophe are terrible to behold. These are the moments when words fail us. You can only weep and there is no reassurance. There is no explanation to give, no message that it will 'all be better soon'. 'Be silent,' says Zephaniah. Nothing will save you, there is no sense to be made of this; there is nothing that will help you see.

I will bring such distress upon people that they shall walk like the blind. (Zephaniah 1.17)

The mistake we make in reading apocalypse is to assume that this is a kind of prophecy, a description of events we will be able to observe and catalogue. That really is not what is going on here. This is writing that tries to express something of the enormity of what happens to us when our powers of description and explanation fail us. This is the day when everything goes dark. It is impenetrable, mysterious. Later in these texts, in different passages, there might well be words of reassurance and a new hope, but this was never a story in which one thing sensibly follows another. It is discontinuous. You shut one book. You fall silent. You pick up another. It is a new story.

That insight is part of what we have to grapple with at Advent. Our imagination cowers. Yes, of course we are people of hope. The same God who created us is the God who redeems us and the God whose kingdom comes. That, though, is his story and not ours to catalogue or control. The truth is that we have no handle on the sheer scale and sweep of God's nature and purpose. Put simply, we do not know God.

I once made that point – 'we do not know God' – in a sermon on the Trinity. A very irritated lady took several days about it but she came to see me and ticked me off in no uncertain terms. 'You need to go back to Bible school,' she said. Indeed, I think she might even have called me 'laddie'. At the risk of offending her (and you), I will say it again. Christians are the people who do not know God. It is essential, if our theology or our prayers are to be honest, that we acknowledge that we do not know God. We cannot explain, we do not comprehend, we will not understand. Here is Austin Farrer (he was beginning a sermon on predestination):

> I am not going to make you see how difficult it is. I am going to make you look into the unfathomable abyss of God's will; and if you turn away with a dizzy head, you will at least have looked beneath the surface of things.[4]

God is not *like* anything and all comparisons will fail. God's glory and grace cannot be mapped any more than we can measure infinity, or eternity. One of the things that should happen in Advent is that we acknowledge that.

That, however, does not help us very much. Mysteriousness is all very well, but it is not always *satisfying*. I too like Advent; one of my favourite moments of the liturgical year comes when we turn off the lights in the cathedral on Advent Sunday and wait to hear a voice sing, from the most distant chapel to the east of us, the Advent Matin Responsory:

> I look from afar:
> And lo, I see the power of God coming, and a cloud covering the whole earth.

I always savour that moment. Then, when the service ends, I routinely have a conversation with someone frustrated that we began a service with something you could hardly hear in a building in which it was very hard to see. The Advent antiphon works for me because I know the text (so I do not need the light on, nor do I have to look at the service sheet) and I know what comes next and why it comes next. It works for me because I have some understanding.

The *first* thing we have to say is that 'we do not know God'. The *second* thing we have to say (or perhaps, better still, the second part of the first thing) is that we *do* know Jesus Christ, and knowing him we are given a lifetime's understanding and explanation. It is precisely his lifetime that is the explanation, and it will serve for all of ours. We tell the story of Jesus Christ, of his birth, life, teaching and example, of his death and resurrection. We tell that story because we think it gathers up every other story. This is the story of everything, for ever. In Advent, we just make a beginning; we sketch out a few hints about *before* and *after*. Then we tell the story of the life of Christ. We talk about John the Baptist, the Virgin Mary and her cousin Elizabeth, and the rest of the story follows in the course of the Christian year. Each year tells the story again. We take a long look back and forward to horizons we cannot describe. Then we tell the story of Jesus Christ because it helps us to understand. We tell his story because we know it is not over.

It is not enough to speak of a mystery we cannot penetrate. We do need to acknowledge that we are working (like those prophets) at the limits of what we can describe, but we also need to be clear that there is indeed a narrative to help us. At the heart of Advent is the conviction that the story of God's grace began in creation and is not over. This is the fundamental idea we need to grasp as we make our way through the Christian year. In the midst of lives that sometimes seem unsatisfactory and confronted by events that bring us near despair, we keep telling a story about a God who is the beginning and the end, a God who creates and who will redeem. We are haunted by a fear that it might all come to nothing, that we were born without purpose and might die without meaning. The story Christians tell is that whatever the evidence to the contrary, God will gather up every loose end. Nothing will be lost; nothing will be meaningless. This is the scale and sweep with which Advent deals. This is the future for which Advent hopes.

Between now and not yet

Advent hopes; it does not expect. Expectation always has to be reasonable, it must be plausible. I cannot reasonably say, 'I expect the fountains in the city will pour forth fine claret this afternoon.' So, expectation is always cautious. I might, however, *hope* that there will be claret. Hope can be extravagant. Real hope overturns what most of us merely *expect*. In truth, claret from fountains is probably more of an ideal daydream, and in all sorts of ways it would be very messy. Real hope, Christian hope, has more bone and substance than that, but it is still always better than what we merely expect. Christian hope is startling. In Advent that is precisely what we are told. In a reading at the heart of the Advent carol service, we hear the great promise made by Isaiah. We are reminded that we do not know God:

> To whom then will you liken God,
> or what likeness compare with him? (Isaiah 40.18)

Then, the size and scale of our hope is set out:

> those who wait for the LORD shall renew their strength,
> they shall mount up with wings like eagles,
> they shall run and not be weary,
> they shall walk and not faint. (Isaiah 40.31)

In the same service, we might hear John the Baptist quoting Isaiah and proclaiming, 'Prepare the way of the Lord, make his paths straight' (Mark 1.3). That is a measure of how startling

Advent is. John said this in the Judean desert, a place of pin-
nacles, cliffs and ravines. Any journey there is full of twists
and turns. Yet there, in the very last place you might imagine,
John declares that there will be a royal highway, a straight road
through all the contours. You can read about how that might
work in the book of Baruch:

> God has ordered that every high mountain and the everlast-
> ing hills be made low and the valleys filled up, to make level
> ground, so that Israel may walk safely in the glory of God.
> (Baruch 5.7)

John imagines a very different future: one glimpse of a world
where God and creation are finally, fully reconciled.

John announces that hope, and then we meet Jesus. Jesus
appears, we are told, *in those days*. This is a phrase the evangelist St Mark uses in order to tell the time. Knowing what time
it is, knowing that the time has come, is crucially important.
Jesus declares,

> The time is fulfilled, and the kingdom of God has come
> near . . . (Mark 1.15)

Telling the right time is important because Jesus announces
that although we live in the present, the future has come near.
That is what happens in *those days*. In all that follows, he
continues to steer a course between *now* and *not yet*. It is
this space between *now* and *not yet* that is the landscape of
Advent.

Jesus taught in parables that described the future. 'The
kingdom of God is like,' he says, and offers an illustration.
He saw the future in very familiar things: the kingdom is like
a wedding, a field, a seed. Yet that sure confidence, that he
knew the future and could describe it, was tempered by the
conviction that it had not yet arrived. The future has yet to
come and we are not ready. Like bridesmaids who fail to light
lamps, or like an improperly dressed guest, we fluff our cues.

The kingdom of God's future is always close at hand and, nonetheless, still at a remove. There is more of the story to follow. The very landscape will be changed and we too must be altered.

We must change. The future requires something from us:

> The time is fulfilled, and the kingdom of God has come near; repent, and believe in the good news. (Mark 1.15)

Repent (*metanoein*) means 'change your mind', and more besides. It is better understood as 'turn round', or even 'go back again'. This is how Jesus begins his preaching. In Mark's Gospel, these are the first words we hear from him. The kingdom has come near and we must think again, turn round, face the other way. We must *repent*. There is so much that ties us to the way things are, to the world as it is. While we may not be completely happy with the way things are, we do at least know where we fit in. We conform to the world as it is. To find our way into the future, however, we must let go, turn round. We must *repent*. We seem to have almost forgotten that Advent is a season of repentance. It is a time to turn.

The turning around is radical. Here is Lancelot Andrewes:

> First, a 'turn', wherein we look forward to God, and with our 'whole heart' resolve to turn to Him. Then a turn again wherein we look backward to our sins wherein we have turned from God, and with beholding them our very heart breaketh. These two are two distinct, both in nature and names; one, conversion from sin; the other, contrition for sin. One resolving to amend that which is to come, the other reflecting and sorrowing for that which is past. One declining from evil to be done hereafter; the other sentencing itself for evil done heretofore. These two between them make up a complete repentance, or to keep the word of the text, a perfect revolution.[5]

Putting it right

This is the language with which Advent starts and it is where we must begin. We must know our limits, accepting that there is much we do not know. We live in hope, not expectation. We acknowledge that if our hope is to be fulfilled then all things must change, including us. So, Advent is a season of repentance. Understand that and we can begin to make sense of what Advent has to tell us about the painful business of putting things right.

We know about the wrongness of the world and the people in it. We know about injustice, violence, cruelty and pollution. On a good day, we might even acknowledge what is wrong with us. We know what needs putting right. In scripture, this putting right is described as *judgement*. All that is evil will be identified and set apart, one thing told from another. The story that is so important to us will have the right ending. The Christ we look for in Advent will come as Judge.

Judgement, though, is an uncomfortable thing to hope for. There are difficulties here. A good friend of mine has Welsh ancestors. One of them, a great-great-grandfather, was the Revd Dr Henry Harries, a Welsh Baptist minister and a preacher of the hell and damnation kind. He seemed actively to look forward to the great judgement. If you have ever listened to Verdi's *Requiem* you will know that there is wonderful, urgent music when you get to the *Dies Irae*. The *Dies Irae* are the 'days of wrath', and few of us would share Verdi's enthusiasm. My friend has the manuscript of some of Harries' sermons; a rather splendid inheritance. Unfortunately, they are in Welsh and my friend cannot read them. In truth, he is only where most of us are. Judgement, as in the Last Judgement, is foreign to us. It is the problem of now and not yet. We are in the midst of the story, and not only do we not know how it will turn out, we cannot *imagine* how it will turn out. We cannot conceive of the way a compromised world will be put right, or know how the loose ends will be gathered in. The images we have – Christ seated on a rainbow with a sword, the saved going one way while the damned are dragged, gibbering, in another – do not resolve the difficulty. Judgement beggars the imagination.

Death is the wrong ending

Our difficulty comes from a kind of impatience. Anyone who reads detective fiction knows that the story will be ruined if you look at the last chapter. You have to sit with the story. If you do jump ahead to the last chapter you will find that you have not just ruined the story. You will also be lost, without the detail that got you there; some of the story will not make sense. The discipline of Advent is patience, it is the discipline of living in the midst of the now and not yet. Advent is the promise that the story will be properly told, evil will be confounded, but that the solution is not ours to deliver. Advent hopes, it does not expect. Advent does not rush to judgement and nor should we.

We began with a walk in Wells and a faltering conversation about dying. I think now not just about Michael Perham but also about my mother, who died a few days before I wrote a first draft of this chapter. Her last years were clouded by dementia and a loss not only of memory but of vocabulary. Her life was increasingly one of unfinished sentences. Even before she died, she and I began to experience bereavement. It was not just sep-aration, but the strong sense that this was the wrong end to the story. It is what death does; it always leaves us with things not said, hopes unfulfilled, experiences not shared. Death is always the wrong ending; there are always unfinished sentences. The promise of Advent is that whatever our experience there is a narrative and even our loose endings are gathered in.

That means that Advent brings us face to face with our lim-its, it plunges us into uncertainty. The word 'Advent' comes from the same root as the word adventure. These weeks before Christmas are supposed to feel like a roller-coaster ride. That is why, perhaps, the Church has struggled to decide how long Advent should last. We have fairly recently added a 'Kingdom' season as a way of getting a grip on this uncertain and unsettling time. The truth is that we are supposed to feel the uncertainty, feel loose on our moorings, in Advent. The baby born in Bethlehem may look small, safe and familiar, but this child will live our life once and for all; he will live a human life *definitively*. Christ lives our lives so that we can see what living really looks like. He is what we must (and will) become. He is the test of whether or not we have lived fully and the promise of the fulfilment to come. He is the judge of what we should be. He is the life we will live.

Most of us spend Advent trying hard to make Christmas safe, make it manageable. We tie Christmas up with ribbon and put it under the tree ahead of the day. We truss it up and have it ready in the fridge. It is not wrong to prepare for Christmas; if you are going to celebrate, you have to get ready. Advent, though, is the season when we are supposed to be reminded that the future is not what we make it, but what God gives us. It is the season in which it is Christ, not us, who will judge what has been done well. Advent is the gathering in of the lost and the completing of unfinished sentences.

Advent is the season when we give the future back to God. In Wells on that November day, Michael Perham summoned all his courage and did just that.

Notes

1 M. Perham, *Glory in Our Midst* (London: SPCK, 2005), p. 11.

2 M. Perham, *The Way of Christ-Likeness* (Norwich: Canterbury Press, 2016), pp. 146–7.

3 Perham, *Glory in Our Midst*, p. 7.

4 A. Farrer, *The Essential Sermons* (London: SPCK, 1991), p. 189.

5 L. Andrewes, 'A Sermon for Ash Wednesday 1619' in *Ninety-Six Sermons by Lancelot Andrewes*, Vol. 1 (Oxford, 1851), p. 359.

Christmas
Telling the wrong story

The meaning of Christmas

There are moments of silence in Advent when we look and listen for a greater glory. Christmas is different; Christmas bustles in, wearing baubles and waving a cracker. It is distracted and more than a bit brash: pubs with Christmas playlists, reindeers leaping on jumpers, miles of tinsel and all that 'ho-ho-hoing'. For some of us, of course, Christmas is quiet and it can be very lonely, but the public Christmas is big, bright and bumptious. Always and everywhere, it shouts out at us; it wants our attention. We complain about that. I have discovered, over the years, that at Christmas you have a simple choice. Either tell 'the vicar' that 'This is your busy time of year', or say to anyone who will listen, 'Christmas is not what it used to be.' There are so many earnest conversations about the real 'meaning' of Christmas.

Now, of course, something has gone badly wrong when Christmas becomes a festival of spending money we cannot really afford. We should notice that people are trying to sell us a branded happiness. We should wonder if that could ever really succeed. Even so, if we want to 'keep' Christmas, if we want to get to the heart of Christmas, we must welcome all the confusions and distractions. The 'real meaning' of the season is to be found precisely in its confusions. Christmas is a *both/and* season.

Once a year, I serve my turn as an 'advisor' at one of the three-day selection panels where the Church of England tests vocations to the priesthood. We are called 'advisors' because we give *advice* to bishops who will make the final decisions. The point being, you can 'advise' a bishop, you can never 'direct' him or her (this is a particularly important bit of learning if you happen to be a dean). I have done this for a while and some of the conversations I have had made a particular impression. One of my tasks is to be clear that a candidate has a *resilient* faith and can handle difficulty. In front of me, some years ago, was a woman in her thirties. I already knew some of her story: she had been widowed, her husband having died after a lengthy illness, and she had small children to love and look after. I was a bit wary of trespassing on to painful ground, but it became pretty clear, pretty quickly, that I was in the presence of a rare resilience. This lady was remarkably composed and happy to tell the story. I listened. She described a day in hospital when she and the medical staff had acknowledged that there really was nothing more that could be done and that death was probably not far off. As that conversation ended, she started gathering up her children and their things. 'What are you going to do now?' she was asked. She explained that she needed to go shopping because there was no food in the house and she shepherded the children down to the hospital car park. By the time she arrived at the supermarket, there was someone waiting for her, asking for her by name. 'Give us your shopping list, we will do that for you. Take your children to the café, we will pay for your meal.'

She told the story as an illustration of being able to find light in the darkness. She told it cheerfully and I only hope she did not notice that I suddenly seemed curiously preoccupied with my notes, because I was more emotional than she was. That act of kindness, a hospital ringing a supermarket, someone in a supermarket seizing the moment, did not alter the terrible inevitability of a terminal illness. The days ahead were still terrible. There was, though, that day a glimpse of something else, another story to tell. The world was just the same and yet it was also different: *both/and*.

It is exactly what the Gospels are trying to tell us. Christmas carols can seduce the faithful into thinking that the baby in the manger arrives to the sound of trumpets and drums. Singing about angels from the realms of glory, or hearing an organ and a choir belt out the glory and embassy of herald angels, we are too easily persuaded that:

> The world in solemn stillness lay,
> To hear the angels sing.[1]

It was not like that. The Christmas story has *always* been full of bustle and bravado. There has been a great kerfuffle and attention has always been pulled in other directions. When Christ was born, the surrounding din was overwhelming. The *real* Christmas was not a still and silent night. We have always been asked to see one thing, and another. It is *both/and*. We need to be clear that it is *both/and*. We might feel as though Christmas is crying out to be organized (lists, a timetable and agreement about who is preparing the Brussels sprouts). The truth is that it is a mistake to try to tidy all this up. In Advent, we should have learnt something about truths not easily put into words. At Christmas, we need to hold our nerve and still resist the temptation to make it simpler than it is.

The wrong story – Luke

Go to church at Christmas and more often than not you will hear either St John saying that 'the Word was with God, and the Word was God' (John 1.1), or St Luke telling us, 'In those days a decree went out from Emperor Augustus . . .' (Luke 2.1). Two contrasting statements, two contrasting styles; but these are just two different ways of saying exactly the same thing.

We will start with Luke. It is worth noting, in passing, that Luke's Gospel does not start with Christmas. This is not a biography and it does not begin with a birth. That is because Luke has something else in mind. Before we ever get to the manger, he has given a great sweep of history and a startling cast of characters. We have visited Jerusalem, Nazareth and the

Judean hills. We have had the Old Testament quoted (many times). We have met an announcing angel (twice), a priest and his wife (and their neighbours), and we have been introduced to Joseph, and Mary. We have heard about King Herod, the Emperor Augustus, and Quirinius, the governor of Syria. Luke is determined that we will understand that the birth of Christ is an event that happens in the midst of a drama involving nations, governments and faiths. We should notice that while it all sounds very much like history, no dates are provided for us. Luke is more interested in the names of people and places – Augustus, Quirinius, Nazareth, Bethlehem . . . He does not want us to think about months and years, but about the Jewish Temple, the Roman emperor and the prefect of Judea. Luke wants us to know that Jesus was born into a world where orders were being shouted, where the weak obeyed the strong and the strong feared the emperor. This is politics more than it is history; we are being prompted to think about uniforms and swords, about plans and broken promises. We can easily overlook some of the details that would have stood out once. Mention of Augustus would have made contemporaries think about that name and what it means. Gaius Octavius, called *Augustus*. The word means 'to increase', and the man did his best to live up to that calling. He was ambitious. He was voracious.

Contemporaries would have known too about the *Pax Augusta*: the golden age of peace that he claimed to have secured and named. If they were particularly well informed, they might even know that while this increasing emperor talked about his peace, he still managed to annex Egypt, invade the Balkans and conquer Spain. Augustus spoke softly and carried a very big stick.

Luke wants us to notice that Jesus was born into *this* world, into its violence and its dodgy rhetoric, into divided loyalties and mistrust. He was born into a very complicated family with its own issues of trust. Luke has deliberately set the hares running. He has begun one story about the Temple being a place of barren despair (we begin with an old priest called

Zechariah who is childless; he is the symbol of a hope that has failed). Then, he has started another narrative about the nations and great leaders in their pomp and pride. Even the census that requires Joseph and Mary to travel to Bethlehem is politically charged. Faithful Jews knew that King David had once commanded a census. He did that in order to measure his own magnificence. He had to be sharply reminded that all things belong to God, not to the king. A census was the worst kind of self-aggrandizement, and scripture takes a dim view of possessiveness.

These are not inconsequential details. This is not just a little added colour for our Christmas story. This is a deliberate counterpoint: one story set against another, and both are important. We are so good and clever at Christmas, we are so familiar with it. We are so good at spotting the baby in the manger, the star in the sky, the herald angels. We have forgotten that the wise men got lost and had to stop and ask. We have forgotten that there was no room at the inn. We have forgotten that the angels went and sang to the wrong sort of people (shepherds were not the kind of people you invited to come and meet your mother), because no one else was listening. In fact, the three Gospel readings set for Christmas originate from the three Christmas Masses. The Gospel set for midnight ends as the angels exult. We don't even get to the manger. The dawn Mass brings the shepherds to the cradle, as we inch slowly nearer to the truth. The Gospel for the Mass of the day is John, at which point the light has dawned. There is a doctrinal point being made in this sequence.

At Christmas, as described by Luke, God appears and nearly everyone is looking the other way. In the midst of a prevailing narrative about power and religion, God arrives powerless, a baby in a manger. Into a world that thought peace was what you got if you had an army to keep you safe, the Prince of Peace arrives and he has no weapons at all. So, the angels singing over the shepherds' field deploy a delicious irony when they speak of peace to God's people on earth. The emperor might tell himself that he had secured a peace and named that peace after himself, but it was not a true and deep peace. Into a story about possessions (that story of the census), God breaks in and God is homeless and impoverished. We are supposed to notice all this. We are supposed to notice that we tell one story and God tells another. We keep telling the *wrong* story.

The wrong story – John

It is precisely the point being made in the beginning of John's Gospel. Again, this is not the story we expect to read. This time there are not even any angels, there are no shepherds, no wise men. What John writes sounds much more like philosophy: 'In the beginning was the Word'. It is serious stuff, dense and thoughtful, but John knows just as well as Luke that Christ is born into a world of muscle, violence, celebrity and opinion. It is a dark and dangerous world, so John keeps talking about light. It is a world that is fascinated by the wrong story. That is why John tells us:

> He was in the world, and the world came into being through him; yet the world did not know him. He came to what was his own, and his own people did not accept him. (John 1.10–11)

John knows, just as Luke knows, that we are easily distracted. He knows that we are surrounded by voices competing for our attention. In John, a word is spoken, but not heard; light dawns, but the darkness does not make way.

Paradox

We are so easily distracted by things that loom large, like power, or possessions. We look to these things not just because they catch our eye but because they are the frame of reference. Power and possessions are the way we understand the world; these are the forces that drive events, they make things happen. Power and possessions are at the heart of the story we always tell. It is one story, but it is not the only story. Christmas begs to differ.

At Christmas, while the world is looking elsewhere, a pregnant girl arrives, unnoticed, in a hill town on the edge of an empire. No accommodation is made for her; she merits no attention. Later, a motley group of shepherds (those people you tried to avoid) come to find her and her child. This rather shabby scene, despite every appearance to the contrary, is the story in which God shows himself. This is the truth that we can so easily overlook. With Mary, close by the crib, we can begin to look at the world and ourselves in a very different way. The old story (the one about power and possessions) rattles on oblivious, but here there is a different understanding of peace and power (Matthew makes the magi kneel down in front of Christ, in case we have not noticed how authority is being subverted). Here, our desperate need to take control is challenged as God works out our salvation in contingency and risk. Here, the big philosophical questions that John juggles with take shape. In the fourth century, a staggeringly learned theologian, Gregory of Nazianzus, struggled to put into words distinctions that cannot be contained:

> The laws of nature are overcome . . . He Who is not carnal is Incarnate; the Son of God becomes the Son of Man . . . O strange conjunction; the Self-Existent comes into being, the Uncreated is created, That which cannot be contained is contained . . . And He Who gives riches, becomes poor . . . What are the riches of His Goodness? What is this mystery that is around me?[2]

Another fourth-century theologian, Ephrem the Syrian, described the confusion that Mary might have felt, wondering how to address her own child. 'Should I call thee Son? . . . Lord should I call thee?'[3] Artists too have struggled with the topsy-turvy truth of Christmas. It is why we see such improbably mature babies holding themselves upright on Mary's lap to bless kneeling kings. How do you paint the invisible God suddenly made visible in a child? As Neil MacGregor, the former director of the National Gallery, wryly observed, 'Paradox is easy to write, but hard to paint.'[4]

We can look, or we can go on being distracted. There is a sideshow at Christmas that works so hard that it looks like the main event. It is exactly as it should be. It has always been important to tell *that* story and know that there is another one.

Christmas asks us if we will believe that a baby can bear the weight of glory. Christians are the people who know the answer to that question is 'Yes', but Christians need to feel, and go on feeling, the gobsmacked improbability of their belief. There is a wonderful irony in the fact that now thousands come to our cathedrals at just this time of year. The thing that we should notice about the baby in Bethlehem is how few there were who acknowledged his arrival and how far some of them had to come. The eye-catching, attention-grabbing story is the one about an emperor, a world that crushed dissent and called it 'peace', a census, and a murderous king. All those assumptions would be challenged by the baby in the manger, but virtually no one was listening and the threat he posed looked laughable. It looked laughable still when he was nailed to a cross.

The human life of Jesus, born of Mary (and ours, if we follow him), can be the place where God is seen and known. Christ's human life is the *only* place where God is seen and known (there are other encounters with God, but *seeing* and *knowing* would not be the right words for them). The human life of Christ is our lens on the life of God. When we see Christ teach, when we see him heal, or sit at table, when we see Christ judged, condemned, abused and dying, we must say that 'God is like this'. It is the story we have to keep telling, but we must acknowledge the implausibility of what we say, the paradox in our faith. It is an idea captured by Elizabeth Jennings in a poem not about Christmas but about the annunciation.

It is a human child she loves
Though a god stirs beneath her breast
And great salvations grip her side.[5]

As the Swiss theologian Hans Urs von Balthasar puts it, God is 'love and surrender' and Jesus is what that looks like. Love and surrender were born in Bethlehem while the legions of the empire slept behind their fortress doors.

After weeks of public clamour, when the day comes, we tame Christmas; we truss it up with tinsel and make it a domestic feast celebrated at fireside and table. We are not entirely wrong. It is indeed the 'human' things that should get our attention. God meets us here in the one form we are most likely to recognize. He comes among us as one of us. Politics, economics and even faith all claim *success*, but it is the vocation to be human, really human, fully human, that confronts us at Christmas. If we make any mistake in all the fun, it is in trying to wrestle control into our own hands and make Christmas another of our successes. Christmas becomes a bit of a tyranny when it has to be done the way we did it last year and the year before, or when it has to be perfect. God meets us in Christ's life; it is Christ who shows us what human living looks like. It was not and will never be quite what we thought.

Notes

1 Edmund Sears, 'It came upon the midnight clear' (poem and carol, 1849).

2 Gregory Nazianzus, *Oration* 38.

3 Ephrem, Rhythm the Eleventh.

4 N. MacGregor, *Seeing Salvation: Images of Christ in Art* (London: BBC, 2000), p. 13.

5 E. Jennings, 'The Annunciation' in *Collected Poems* (London: Carcanet Press, 1986), p. 45.

3

Epiphany
Looking at the stars

How much can you see?

In a small museum in Winterthur, just outside Zurich, there
is a painting of the *Adoration of the Kings* by Pieter Bruegel.
You will, almost certainly, have seen other pictures of the adoration. Artists like Epiphany. They seize upon this scene as an
opportunity to play with the idea of majesty. They tempt us
with the finery of the kings and taunt us with the poverty of
the setting. The gifts, the gold, some splendid casket or other,
all add to the dash and dazzle of the day. The baby, by contrast, is often naked. Bruegel knew all about those tricks, and
in London there is a very unsettling *Adoration* by him in which
the defenceless baby writhes away from the gift of myrrh. But
go to Winterthur, and you must set those ideas aside. This is
something else: a picture of a snowstorm. Heavy flakes swirl
about a village already deep in snow. Anything that is not
white is brown. The palette of colours is much reduced, and
detail is hard to pick out. The scene is busy; there must be 80
figures or more, though you have to peer through the snow
to see them. It is a muddle, this painting; there is no obvious
focus. If you did not know the title, you would be hard pressed
to make any sense of what is before you. Look closely, though,
take your time, and you will see that in one corner of this
slightly hectic scene the figures are still. Two men kneel before
a seated woman. It is here, off centre and almost out of focus,
that the glory of God is finally to be found. This misdirection,

this confusion, is a trick that Bruegel played often. In his wonderful *Procession to Calvary* in Vienna it will take you a few moments to find the figure of Christ carrying his cross. This artist is a master of painting pictures that ask the viewer, 'Do you see?' He is the painter who reminds us that the gospel is worked out in the midst of things, when we might be looking the other way. It was Bruegel who prompted Auden to write the poem 'Musée des Beaux Arts', and observe that drama and tragedy occur while so many of us are preoccupied. Bruegel knew that even the King of kings could be overlooked, while (as Auden put it), 'dogs go on with their doggy life'. He asks if we know that too, asks if we are paying attention. Do you see?

Epiphany poses that same question in a very striking way. Epiphany wonders how much, how far, we can see. Christmas insists that the distractions are real, that there is a tension between the way we do things and the way God works. Christmas knows that both God and the world demand attention. Epiphany, however, puts Christ front and centre and challenges us to see as we should. As Christmas ends, with bodies beached on sofas, some of them anaesthetized with alcohol, Epiphany arrives. Now, we catch hold of the coat-tails of glory and have to hang on tight. God is seen in the manger; the question is, will God be named, acknowledged and worshipped? If you ask the clergy about Epiphany, they will look thoughtful, stroke their chins and tell you that *Epiphany* is a Greek word and it means *manifestation*. At Epiphany God is made *manifest*: that is, God is *made plain*. We either see that, or we don't.

Years ago, Romans fixed Christmas on 25 December. Egypt, meanwhile, had a different calendar, and the feast day was 6 January. Back in Rome, working on the excellent principle that two feasts are always better than one, both 25 December and 6 January were put into the calendar. In a way, that gave us Christmas twice over. Epiphany in the East, however, was always an altogether richer, more complicated thing than our Christmas. It was always more than a celebration of a birth: the anniversary, as it were, of a thing that happened. Epiphany, remember, means *manifestation*. Christmas concentrates our gaze on the baby in the manger, the scandal of a God who might so easily be overlooked (the risk of telling the wrong story). Epiphany is not so focused on just the one event; it is much more interested in seeing what difference this makes. At Epiphany, we hear about wise men kneeling at the crib. We also hear about the baptism of Christ, when the heavens opened, and we go to Cana, where Christ turned water into wine.

If you go to a service on the Feast of the Epiphany, 6 January, it is quite likely that you will only hear about the three kings. Epiphany, though, has been turned (fairly recently) from a day into a season. On the Sundays of Epiphany, we are asked to range more broadly. The length and richness of this full season of Epiphany may be modern, but it is interesting; there is a danger that without it we will miss the point. There is a lot to say, but we do need to begin with the kings. Julie Andrews was not wrong; you have to begin at the very beginning:

> In the time of King Herod, after Jesus was born in Bethlehem of Judea, wise men from the East came to Jerusalem. (Matthew 2.1)

The beginning, the setting, is important. Once again, the geography, politics and history are all significant. Bethlehem, Judea, Jerusalem – Matthew reels off the place names. He tells us about Herod and gives us our bearings within the history books. He then gives us wise men (*magi* is what Matthew calls them; they are certainly not kings, they are astrologers, and it is no accident that they follow a star). Soon, we are dealing with complicated negotiations between these magi and King Herod. And there is more. The magi are Gentiles, not Jews; they have come from the East, beyond Judea. So, when these foreigners kneel at the crib, we see that this child is not just the Messiah promised to the Jews. This is the Lord who will be acknowledged by all nations: the Saviour of the world.

We are still not finished; we must add into the mix the fact that astrology only gets them so far. They follow a star, but they get lost. It brings them to Jerusalem and then it lets them down. They are reduced to asking questions in the streets and only pick up the trail again when they hear the voice of prophecy in scripture. Prophecy is more reliable than astrology.

> And you, Bethlehem, in the land of Judah, are by no means least among the rulers of Judah; for from you shall come a ruler who is to shepherd my people Israel. (Matthew 2.6)

Matthew is interested in prophecy. He insists, over and again, that prophecy has been 'fulfilled'. He points us to prophecy, but also occasionally slips in the voice of the prophets without making any comment, or waving any flag to make sure we notice. He has done just that in this story. As the magi produce their gifts, an alert reader might just hear echoes of Isaiah and the psalmists. We have heard about this moment long ago:

> all those from Sheba shall come.
> They shall bring gold and frankincense,
> and shall proclaim the praise of the LORD. (Isaiah 60.6)

> May the kings of Tarshish and of the isles render him tribute,
> may the kings of Sheba and Seba bring gifts.
> May all kings fall down before him, all nations give him service. (Psalm 72.10–11)

Very deliberately, Matthew is telling us one story, a narrative about three magi who travel to meet a newborn baby, and also an altogether bigger tale that sweeps up politics and places, astrological speculation and prophecies. Here, all the great purposes of God swing, like the stars, round Bethlehem. As the story unfolds, it takes in fear and violence as Herod launches a tide of blood. And there is yet more prophecy:

> Then was fulfilled what had been spoken through the prophet Jeremiah: 'A voice was heard in Ramah, wailing and loud lamentation, Rachel weeping for her children.' (Matthew 2.17–18)

When we talk about Epiphany as *manifestation* what we mean is that God is made manifest, is seen, in the midst of all this drama. God is seen in places we can name, in our history and in the mess and muddle of life.

Narrow down the glory

The point we need to grasp is that the story of Jesus Christ is not just *seen* in the midst of things, but it *explains* all those things. This is the story that embraces everything else. In the splendidly economical words of the *Catechism of the Catholic Church*, 'God has said everything in his Word.' The catechism goes on to quote the sixteenth-century Carmelite friar and poet John of the Cross:

> In giving us his Son, his only Word (for he possesses no other), he spoke everything to us at once in this sole Word – and he has no more to say . . .[1]

It is what the Gospels are trying to tell us, and Epiphany insists upon the point. Partially, of course, we are being reminded that what we meet in Christ is *sufficient* for us. We need nothing more. More than that, though, Christ is the origin and end of all things. He is the Word, which explains all things.

Epiphany and the encounter with Christ must, as a result, always act as a summons to us. It is always going to require a response from us, for it is an encounter with the *all* of God. God's glory and God's purposes are here, contained in the manger, acknowledged at the Jordan, and glimpsed at Cana. So, if we are ever to truly *see* Christ we have to see him whole, see God's glory and God's purposes. Christ was indeed a baby in a manger, he was a boy who travelled from Nazareth to Jerusalem with his parents, but he was always also the King of the nations, the Prince of Peace, the Word that was spoken at the beginning. Christian faith will always be a call to go out from where we are. It will never be an invitation to bring down the shutters.

It is John, perhaps, who makes the point most forcefully. At Christmas, we heard what sounds like a rather bewildering take of the birth of Christ:

In the beginning was the Word, and the Word was with God, and the Word was God. (John 1.1)

Without being too technical about Greek philosophical terms and the way we translate them, it might help if we understand this phrase as saying: 'In the beginning was the *explanation*.' That is what John is driving at. The Word that exists from the very beginning is the Word that describes God. God is neither self-contained nor self-absorbed. From the very beginning, God pours out in explanation. A Word of explanation is spoken, and the explanation is Jesus. Put another way, God tells us the story about absolutely everything, and the story turns out to be Jesus Christ. His life, death and resurrection, his refusal to abuse power, his generosity, his love of the poor, his ability to forgive, his healing touch, his surprising life, is the explanation of everything. Jesus Christ is the story of everything that is and the story of everything that was and is still to be.

There is a poem by the priest and poet David Scott called 'Reading Party'. Gently, it pokes fun at a group of clergy who go on retreat in the Lake District and are abashed by the scale of the scenery. They look for something familiar, a little more comforting, 'to narrow down the glory'.[2] They succumb to a very familiar temptation. When we turn away from political or civic engagement, finding it godless, or somehow irrelevant, when we seek out Christian culture, the music and conversation that *we* know, and when we pray over others without asking them what they need, we tread the same road. We narrow down the glory. There is an abiding temptation to make it all safe and familiar. We want Christ to be human, as we are human. We want to read across into him our experience. When we feel doubt, we want to be sure that he too felt doubt, because we want to claim that our feelings can be trusted. The sustained determination to demonstrate that Jesus must have had a sexual relationship is rooted in a similar conviction that our experience is normative and he must therefore share it. Christ, however, was made like us so that we might become like him. The relationship works the other way round. It is not our experience but his that tells us what we need to know. God shows us (he *manifests*) real humanity in Christ. This is the *everything* about *everything* that God has to say. Christ does not become more human the more we make him feel our own dilemmas. The truth is that we become more human as we follow him. We have a need to make the gospel manageable and so we focus on the personal, on the things we believe we can change. The God made manifest in Christ is always going to burst the constraints we put upon him. God is always going to be active and present in all things, and we will always have to look for him outside what is familiar and safe. The Church does not have God in a box.

It begins with kings but it goes so much further. Matthew says nothing about an inn with no room for guests, nor does he mention a manger. Indeed, he does not describe Jesus' birth at all. All we are told is that the magi came to a house where the child was. We are left in no doubt, however, that this house is a place where all roads meet. Luke tells us a slightly different story about emperors and governors, about war and peace, but makes the same point: history converges at the crib. Mark sets out a *religious* story, about prophets in the wilderness saying 'make straight the way of the Lord', and makes Christ into the future that the world longs to see. All the evangelists agree that when we talk about Christ being made manifest what we mean is that everything falls into place. Here is the picture on the box and now all the pieces of the jigsaw will fit.

God and everything

A few days after the Feast of the Epiphany, on the first Sunday of the season, we come at the story again but this time through the lens of the Baptism of Christ. We are familiar with baptism:

we think of a baby (possibly in lace), an uncle in a tight-fitting suit, proud parents, and relatives hoping there will be plenty to drink later. Baptism is predictable and baptism is a routine. That is a set of associations, however, that sets us off in completely the wrong direction. This baptism is in the wilderness, remember. Baptizers need water, of course, so the wilderness is a strange setting. That is deliberate; the wilderness is the place Israel left behind when Moses died. John the Baptizer, himself born into a family that served the Temple in Jerusalem, is asking the faithful to come out of the cities God gave them and away from their places of worship. He wants them to walk backwards into the story they thought was over.

The very idea of baptism is tricky. Jews are never baptized, they are Jews by *birth*. It is the suggestion that you need to go back to the beginning; it is offensive. This is telling the Jews that they lack real religion, that their faith will not save. In order to be baptized, of course, they have to go down into the water and that too is a challenge. We generally put water in a font and splash a little of it about. John is standing in the kind of water that might turn to flood. Jews think that before creation there was just water, and it was terrifying: 'the earth was a formless void and darkness covered the face of the deep' (Genesis 1.2).

The Jewish view implies that water is the opposite of creation. It is chaotic and meaningless. It is also destructive. Moses got through the sea and then watched it destroy Pharaoh's army.

You blew with your wind, the sea covered them; they sank like lead in the mighty waters. (Exodus 15.10)

That story, the story of Jonah and the whale, the story of Paul's journeys, all depend on the special fear that is to be felt on the sea. When prophets describe a terrifying army, they compare it to the roaring of the sea. So, when 'Jesus came from Nazareth of Galilee' to be baptized with water, when he goes down into the Jordan it looks a bit like dying. It also looks a bit like a new creation, a challenge to the old chaos.

In all this, God is made manifest. The baptism of Christ is so much more than a pious exchange by the side of a river. It is the glory of God and the purposes of God. This is the epiphany we need; we need to see that God speaks in everything, of everything, and does that in Christ. Faith keeps painting itself into a corner. We so often opt for partial explanations that distinguish this from that. We make religion into what sets us apart: *them and us*. We see God in some things and some people. God forgive us, religion turns into what separates us. We manage to sound defeated, defended, divided. God speaks one Word and that Word holds all things together, explains all things. There is just one story; the story of Jesus Christ.

At Christmas, we are tempted to draw the curtains against the cold and either ignore the challenges around us or make it a festival of our own good fortune. At Epiphany, we are invited outside to see the stars and we should gasp at the view.

Notes

1 G. Chapman, *Catechism of the Catholic Church* (London: Continuum, 1995), p. 65.

2 D. Scott, 'Reading Party' in *Selected Poems* (Hexham: Bloodaxe Books, 1998), p. 74.

4

Candlemas
Great expectations

Not going to church

The journalist Michael De La Noy has a famous story about a distinguished and elderly man on a demanding foreign tour. De La Noy was the press secretary bringing news of a cancelled flight. He found the great man lying on a bed, hands clasped behind his white head. He was repeating the words, 'I hate the Church of England. I hate the Church of England.' De La Noy said, 'It's a good thing nobody's here but me to hear you say that.' Michael Ramsey, Archbishop of Canterbury and Primate of All England, replied, 'Oh, but it's true. I do hate the Church of England. Indeed I do.'[1]

There are plenty of people who love religion, but struggle with the Church. The theologian Karl Barth called the Church a 'catastrophe' and used to say that people who think they are on the road to God are just building a church; the very thing that invites you to stop and forget that journey altogether.[2] For Ramsey and for Barth, the Church could appear scandalous, an occasion for despair. For others, it might feel a little less dramatic than that, but just as deadly. The Church can seem just dispiriting and disappointing. C. S. Lewis had his devil, Screwtape, argue that a visitor walking into a church might actually be brought closer to hell itself.

One of our great allies at present is the Church itself . . . When he goes inside, he sees the local grocer with rather an oily expression on his face bustling up to offer him one shiny little book containing a liturgy which neither of them understands, and one shabby little book containing corrupt texts of a number of religious lyrics, mostly bad, and in very small print.[3]

Christians struggle to live up to their calling, but so does the Church. I have met plenty of people who claim to have a Christian faith, but simply cannot bear to go to church. They have tried to persuade me that they could be altogether more authentically *spiritual* if only they could be excused the mess and muddle of church life. Candlemas is the feast that begs to differ.

The seasons that begin the Christian year, Advent, Christmas and Epiphany, are a sustained invitation to leave the shallows and encounter the depth of the glory of God. Advent speaks to us of the last things, death, judgement, heaven and hell; it is a glimpse of the real seriousness of living with consequence. Christmas asks us if we have the courage and imagination to see great truths in small beginnings. Then, Epiphany is the commentary that follows: the conviction that we have indeed seen the glory of God and that this story is good for everyone, everywhere, for ever. Although our Christmas cards often direct us to a little family huddled in a stable, the Gospels are more interested in Rome and Jerusalem, angelic choirs, ancient prophecies and foreign visitors. Christmas and Epiphany will push us out, under the stars, if only we will let them. It is a big canvas and there are broad brush strokes.

Going to the Temple

Candlemas is very different. Candlemas, or the Presentation of Christ in the Temple, or the Purification of the Blessed Virgin Mary, celebrates the moment when Mary and Joseph bring Christ to Jerusalem, 'to present him to the Lord'. So, we go to the Temple. The focus is on a particular place and on a ritual. The purification of a Jewish woman, the presentation of a

child, these are rites of passage: ceremonies in which a community sets its boundaries and describes itself.

> When the time came for their purification according to the
> law of Moses, they brought him up to Jerusalem to present
> him to the Lord. (Luke 2.22)

Mary and Joseph brought Jesus to Jerusalem. Luke seems sure
that they were still staying in Bethlehem at the time. In terms
of distance, Jerusalem was not far away, but their journey took
them from an obscure hill village into one of the greatest cities
of the ancient world. There was a saying, 'Whoever has not
seen Jerusalem in its splendour has never seen a fine city.' Two
buildings in Jerusalem towered over all the others. One was the
Roman fortress, the Antonia, which had been built quite deliberately next to the Temple. The other was the Temple itself,
recently rebuilt by Herod. Visitors would have first glimpsed it
long before they got to the city gates. It was huge, and it was
built not from local stone but from white marble. It shone in
the sun. The walls soared out of the valley floor. The biggest
of the stones used was 12 metres long. Herod had added a
massive colonnade as an entrance. That colonnade alone was
bigger than York Minster. To get to it you had to climb steps
to a height of three storeys, and the steps were cut irregularly,
forcing you to keep breaking your stride. No one could run in,
or out, of the Temple. This was magnificence that was meant
to give you pause.

Go to York Minster, or to St Peter's in Rome, and you
know you are entering a great building and a place of prayer.
Visiting the Temple was that and more. It was not just different in size and scale. To enter the Temple was to trespass on
heaven. It was more than a holy place; faithful Jews believed
that this was God's footstool. This was where heaven touched
earth. There was no suggestion that God was present in
Jerusalem and nowhere else, but God was in the Temple dis-
tinctively and uniquely. Going to the Temple was a pathway
to an encounter:

the spirit lifted me up, and brought me into the inner court; and the glory of the LORD filled the temple . . . I heard someone speaking to me out of the temple. He said to me: Mortal, this is the place of my throne and the place for the soles of my feet, where I will reside among the people of Israel for ever. (Ezekiel 43.5–7)

It is Luke's Gospel that describes this trip to the Temple. That is no accident. Luke was fascinated by Jerusalem and interested in the Temple; he wanted us to think about how and where we look for the presence of God. He begins the Gospel in the Temple, with old Zechariah, and he ends his Gospel at the Temple. Now, he begins this particular story by telling us about the Law that Mary and Joseph should keep, the offering they should make:

according to what is stated in the law of the Lord, 'a pair of turtle-doves or two young pigeons.' (Luke 2.24)

Having got us thinking about ritual and the routines of worship, suddenly Luke shifts our attention away from the purification (the reason that Mary had to go to the Temple). Instead, we are asked to think about the baby and what he might become. The story has a slippery quality about it; is it about Mary, or does it focus on the infant Christ? Is it really about the Temple, or is it about something else? Luke is indeed pointing us elsewhere, and he rather labours his point. Simeon, he says, was looking for 'the consolation of Israel' *and* he is full of the Holy Spirit *and* he has been promised that he would not die before he had seen the Messiah. This is a passage all about expectation and fulfilment. It begins with Mary and Jesus, but it points to the future. Simeon finally sees and rejoices: 'my eyes have seen your salvation' (Luke 2.30). God has kept his promise. In the baby in Simeon's arms we look on the Messiah. It is a glorious moment and it is dripping with irony. We are in the Temple, remember, the place where faithful Jews would go in order to meet the living God. Simeon, however, only finds salvation when a little child is brought in from outside by two people too poor to make the usual offering.

This is how Luke tells us that God is not quite what we thought we believed in. Nor is the Temple the place we thought it was. God is in his own home, but unexpectedly. The building does not determine, or contain, the truth. We are supposed to notice the polarities, not *this*, but *that*. In the darkness – light; in the last times – a new life; and for old, despairing eyes – hope and salvation. Candlemas is the 'unexpectedness' of God. It is a day when hope bustles in, rearranging the furniture. In the legend of St Brendan, this was the day when Judas was allowed out of hell to bathe his torments in the sea. It became a day of processions and candles, all in honour of the light that will 'lighten the Gentiles'.

Our liturgies at Candlemas do their best to pay attention to what happened that day in the Temple. We have, however, latterly become rather taken with the idea that Candlemas is a kind of hinge between Christmas and Lent. Increasingly, churches treat this day as a step change between one season and the next. We look back a little and suggest that this is the end of all that Christmas revelation, all that making *manifest*. Then, we reflect on the last words Simeon speaks, that warning directed to Mary about a sword that 'will pierce your own soul too' (Luke 2.35). That is taken as a hint that we should now turn our gaze towards Lent and the suffering of Passiontide. We have been so taken with the language of *journey* and *pilgrimage* of late that we have emphasized movement from one to another. We inhabit one season, but we stay alert to all the connections with others. We have lengthened Epiphany and made Candlemas serve another purpose. Here, we suggest, is a hinge between the days that celebrate the birth of Christ and the days that herald his death. There are good reasons to do this looking back and looking forwards, but it is perhaps a shame. It does distract our attention from the day itself and its real significance. An earlier generation were interested in what could only be done on this particular day. They thought this day was particular; they did not make it part of something else.

That is what Simeon knew, in the Temple. He knew the significance of the moment. God's presence and God's future rose up before him and he had the grace and courage to see it and to name it. Conventional religion had failed; ritual and piety had not delivered confidence or hope. Simeon was seeking for something more than prayer, he longed for 'the consolation of Israel'. In an occupied territory, with a puppet king, in the midst of a passionate debate about what real faith looked like, he stood in the Temple and hoped for a different future. It is this that makes Candlemas so interesting and so very strange. There, in the text and in the rite, is the warning that trusting too much to the building, or for that matter trusting just in the text and in the rite, we might miss the point. Glory, salvation and light come to Jerusalem but only an old man and an old woman notice. In the Temple the priests and acolytes were looking for something else. Candlemas reminds us that our very faith can confound us. In our better moments, we know that we can be so busy with our worries and our work that we fail to live in faith and hope. Candlemas reminds us that we can also be so busy with our *religion* that we might miss the moment; we might not notice when God has come among us. The King of kings came to the Temple where his name was praised and only Simeon and Anna paused and took note.

Imagining the future, not protecting the past

So, Candlemas is a good moment to take a hard look at the way we think about the Church. Talk about *the Church* and there is an easy assumption, quickly made, that you are probably talking about a large Victorian building just down the road, or perhaps people who go to it. Or, just possibly, you are thinking of bishops, synods and all those boards and agendas that we have. We think of the Church as *this* group of people and *this* place. If, like me, you have a ministry in the Church, you are also inclined to assume that the Church is a community that shares responsibilities and confers duties. Necessary conversations, about things like governance, the management of financial resources and above all (and quite properly) safe-guarding, can quickly persuade us that the Church is a thing we need to sort out, fix, or mend. Soon Church turns into a kind of activity done by a particular set of people. The trouble is that then the activity becomes the preoccupation and churches turn into places of business and not communities of hope. How many hours of my life have I spent counting the number of agenda items we need to flog through while my blood runs dry? I fear that as I die, my last words will be, 'Any other business?'

Simeon looked for 'the consolation of Israel', and he knew, that day in the Temple, that he had glimpsed the future and held the salvation of God in his arms. In a building with a great past he saw a different future. That is the vocation of the Church. Go to a particular church and you may very well find a number of people talking about the way we do things here, or the great days we had. We have a talent, in the Church, for being busy and looking backwards. A few too many rotas, a lit-tle too much effort recreating a moment we think we lost. The truth about the Church, however, is that it is a glimpse of the future. More precisely, it is a glimpse of God's future. Despite our profound concerns for the budget, the Mission Action Plan and the development of lay leadership, it is the future, what we might become, that makes us truly interesting. It is what God will make of us, in his grace and mercy, that makes Christianity compelling. It is so much more than *this* group of people doing *this* thing, *now*. As Clement of Alexandria explained:

> Just as God's will is creation and is called 'the world', so his intention is the salvation of men, and it is called 'the Church'.[4]

The Church is God's future. The Church is the beginnings of the kingdom of God. It is not under our direction and it always points beyond itself. We should always think of and imagine more than we first see when we think of the Church. It is just the insight that Simeon had in the Temple when he saw far beyond the stones and rituals of the Temple. The salvation of Israel had been put into his arms.

The Church is not something we have made, but something we have been given. The Church is, in fact, Christ's gift to us. We are familiar with the idea that the Church is Christ's body (1 Corinthians 12.27). It was his before it was ours. We know that a body has different parts, a head, hands and feet. So, we accept that the Church ought to be various; we should notice variety within it. We can accept that perhaps rather more easily than we can actually live it, but we get the idea. We also have to acknowledge that this is *Christ's* body. Called to follow him, we discover that we need to conform to him, and that to do that we have to live together. Christian vocation is never solitary. Christ is inseparable from the Church. As St Augustine put it:

> If you love but a part, you are divided: if you are divided, you are not in the body; if you are not in the body, you are not under the Head. What profits it you that you believe and blaspheme? Thou adorest Him in the Head, blaspheme Him in the Body.[5]

Of course, the Church is occasionally corrupt, often infuriating, and nearly always a touch uncomfortable. It is full of sinful people like me, and it is the place of encounter where Christ summons me into living and behaving differently. Even so, the Church is necessary; the alternative is more of me and more of the same. The spirituality that would rather avoid Church will always be easier, but it can never be properly Christian because there will not be much of Christ in it.

In our better moments, then, we will acknowledge that the Church is the body of Christ and has a claim on our loyalty. What perhaps we do not always quite understand is that the Church is Christ's *dead* body. As Ephesians explains, 'Christ loved the church and gave himself up for her, in order to make her holy' (Ephesians 5.25–26). His dying on the cross was his gift to us. It is there, in Christ's death, that the Church has its origin. The Church was created on Calvary and its existence rests on what Christ did for us in dying. Only when we have grasped that we are gathered first (before ever we put up a rota, or convene a synod) into the death of Christ, can we finally let go of our over-eager conviction that somehow the Church needs us, or that we have to improve it. The Church is holy, as Ephesians explains, because he made it holy. We do not have to try to make the Church holy as it has been done for us (and we would not do it well). What God has done in Christ is decisive. Michael Ramsey put it like this:

> These events, wrought once for all, are the source of everything that the Christians are and have and know. They are called upon not to advertise their own 'experiences' but to praise God for, and to bear witness to, the historical events wherein the Name and Glory of God were uttered in human flesh.[6]

Simeon instinctively understood that his job was only to announce what had been done for him: 'my eyes have seen your salvation'. He also understood that salvation was linked to suffering. He knew something else, besides. Simeon knew and announced that the promised salvation of God was *for all peoples*. Salvation is generous, and the Church that anticipates that salvation must be generous too.

As the fifth-century French saint Vincent of Lérins put it, the faith of the Church is 'that which has been believed everywhere, always and by all'.[7] It is faith that embraces everyone, everywhere. It may be (in fact it will be) that these particular people, with their particular commitment and their odd foibles, will be the Church here and now, but they do not exhaust what the Church is. Try as it might (and it does try quite hard), the Church can never be exclusive, it cannot be middle class, or male, or conservative. The Church is always more, never less. The shorthand theologians use to make that point is to call the Church *catholic*. The Church can never be less than holy or catholic.

As many of you as were baptized into Christ have clothed yourselves with Christ. There is no longer Jew or Greek, there is no longer slave or free, there is no longer male and female; for all of you are one in Christ Jesus. (Galatians 3.27–28)

We began with a Church that can be dispiriting and disappointing. Here, now, wherever we tip up on a Sunday morning, the Church always appears less than the whole. The Church began in the death of Christ, it is the theatre of Christ's presence and it is our future salvation. We need the hope of Simeon if we are to see in what is before us what we might become.

Notes

1 See https://www.telegraph.co.uk/news/obituaries/1404246/Michael-De-la-Noy.html.

2 S. H. Webb, *Refiguring Theology: The Rhetoric of Karl Barth* (New York: University of New York, 1991), p. 141.

3 C. S. Lewis, *The Screwtape Letters* (London: William Collins, 2016), p. 5.

4 Quoted in G. Chapman, *Catechism of the Catholic Church*, (London: Continuum, 1995), p. 760.

5 Augustine, *Homily X on the First Epistle of John*.

6 M. Ramsey, *The Gospel and the Catholic Church* (Peabody, MA: Hendrickson, 1935, p. 37).

7 Vincent of Lérins, *Commonitory* 2.6.

5

Ash Wednesday
Risking forgiveness

I have already pointed out that modern liturgies think of Candlemas as a turning point in the year, the moment when we leave Christmas and look towards Passiontide. You might find there is a procession leading you from one reality to another and a liturgy that announces, 'We turn from the crib to the cross'. In the cathedral where I work, there was a memorable year when we set off down the nave towards the west end where we would say those words. The head verger (who rather splendidly thinks of liturgy in much the same way as he thinks of grand opera) had arranged a surprise for us. As we reached our destination and the great wooden cross that was now the focus of our thoughts, we were suddenly bathed in a deep purple light. It was the colour of Lent. There was no doubting our change of focus.

Sin and death

A little over 1,000 years ago, a Benedictine abbot, Aelfric of Eynsham, told the story of a man who refused to go to church on Ash Wednesday. Just days later, the man was killed during a boar hunt. Aelfric told that story in an Ash Wednesday sermon. The story did not turn on a sudden death; for Aelfric and his audience that was commonplace and familiar. What made this story startling, what interested Aelfric, was that here was a man who had not taken his chance to repent, and had died in sin. He had died and would not rise again. Here was someone who had died *for ever*.

Lent begins with a day of ashes (*dies cinerum*). Aelfric explains, in a passage that has been quoted over and over again, that the ashes are a sign of repentance of sin:

> Now let us do this little at the beginning of our Lent that we strew ashes upon our heads to signify that we ought to repent of our sins during the Lenten fast.[1]

In Aelfric's time, the idea that Ash Wednesday called us to account for our sins was already familiar. The custom of a Lenten fast began very early indeed, but there was some debate about how long Lent should last. Agreement was reached that a 40-day fast was what was required; as Sundays could not properly be fast days, Ash Wednesday was fixed as the marker for the beginning of a Lenten fast of the right duration. Christians then began to focus something of what they knew about sin and repentance on this particular day. Little by little, Ash Wednesday became a focus for our understanding of Lent and what we think about our own wrongdoing.

Because sin is a liar, and deceitful, you can never be sure where it is, or what it is doing. As I will try to explain, we routinely underestimate sin. We think we can see it and name it and we miss the mark. It is the fundamental characteristic of sin that it misleads and misdirects (which helps to explain why we are so good at seeing it in *other* people, but blind to it in ourselves). It is a bit of a commonplace to suggest that we are not nearly as serious about sin as we were. That is perhaps because we are so thoroughly deceived and have become so confused. We are rather prone to saying that we are no longer serious about sin. In a wonderful aside, the Dominican writer Timothy Radcliffe suggests that part of our problem might not be that we have become indifferent or insensitive to sin, but that we are, in fact, too *anxious*.

> If anything, our society suffers from too much guilt for our failure to be the wonderful parents that our children deserve,

for our wealth and comfort in a global society in which millions die each year of starvation, for our share in the despoliation of the planet. Such guilt, an anguished psychological state rather than an objective recognition of failure, may render us hopeless and helpless. Many people instinctively switch off at any mention of Christianity because they already feel so loaded down with half-suppressed guilt that the last thing they need is to be told that they are sinners.[2]

Our difficulty, he suggests, is that while our guilt looms so large, it is a vague thing and we lack any understanding of repentance, or forgiveness. In generations that came before us sin was properly named; trouble was taken to identify sin. Not only that, sinners were marked out, made visible and then restored. The guilty were excommunicated; some of them could not even enter the church building. One sinner might have her hair cut short, another would wear sackcloth made of goat's hair because she was clearly not a sheep belonging to Christ's flock, and yet another would wear chains (because he was enslaved by sin). This, though, was part of a theology of reconciliation. A community acknowledged what was wrong and a community accepted the remedy. Now, I have no desire to see medieval discipline return (I would be so very embarrassed in sackcloth), but as that culture withered away we slowly lost any understanding of how to navigate our way back into relationships that have been sundered. It is not just that we do not talk about sin. Our more serious failing is that we do not understand reconciliation. We have made sin so private, we hold it close and it is no surprise that we struggle to let go.

Our smudge of ash on Ash Wednesday is the last echo of a former seriousness: a whisper on the breeze that sin and reconciliation might be an issue. Ash is a powerful symbol. When it is used in the liturgy the priest will say over us, 'Remember that you are dust and to dust you shall return.' It is what God said to Adam and Eve when sentence was passed in Eden for their sin. It is also an echo of the funeral service: 'earth to earth, ashes to ashes, dust to dust'. One of the old liturgies for Ash Wednesday pleaded with God to spare those that are penitent:

> Bless and sanctify these ashes that they may be a wholesome medicine to all them that humbly call upon thy holy Name.[3]

Ashes were not just a symbol of the grave. When these customs began you might have used ash as an alternative to soap. Ashes are abrasive, they can make you clean.

So, the liturgy offers a reminder of a time when the language and the actions we used to take account of sin and speak of reconciliation were more vivid and more public. The reckoning of sins and the giving of absolution moved into confessional boxes in the sixteenth century. Piety turned its eyes inwards. Again, we used to think differently. In a reading often heard on Ash Wednesday the prophet Joel summons a fast: 'Blow the trumpet in Zion; sanctify a fast; call a solemn assembly' (Joel 2.15). There is a crisis in Israel and the answer Joel offers is neither a working party nor private prayer. It is a *public* act of sorrow that is required. Everyone has to do this; repentance is an activity for the Church. That is because sin is deadly and sin is public.

Deadly and public: we do not think like that now. Too often Lent begins with us talking about giving up chocolate hobnob biscuits, or perhaps determining to say our prayers for a bit longer. Our engagement with the season and with our own sinfulness turns on a personal discipline. The mistake we make is to think that sin comes from a careless encounter we might have with 'bad things'. We assume that sin is something extra, something that we do, something that we add on. So, sin is an extra helping of sticky toffee pudding, a second bottle of Chateau Langoa Barton. Sin, we think, comes from wanting too much sex or too much money. Sin is an *extra* relationship, a bit, as the saying goes, 'on the side'. That does not sound all that serious. All this talk of the threat from 'bad things' implies that repentance has something to do with giving up what we have added on. Then Lent does indeed become no more than a season without chocolate hobnobs.

There are no bad things

Sin is not like that. Sin is not like that at all. In the first place, there are no bad things. God, remember, made all that is and made all things *good*. We do not have a problem with bad things. We have a problem with desire. If I want a bottle of Chateau Langoa Barton, I really do not want a bad thing. My problem comes when I want it more than I want *other* things. If I want this claret more than I want conversation and company, if I want it more than I want food, or exercise, my desire for this one good thing is out of proportion and it is dangerous. The problem, oddly, is not that I want *too much* (something extra); the problem is that I want *too little*. Shutting the door, drawing the curtains and clutching my glass of claret, I want too few of the gifts that God will give me and I am diminished. Sin is not something extra, sin is always loss. It makes us less than we should be. When Thomas Aquinas wrote about sin, he called it 'a privation of form'. He wanted us to know that it makes us diminished.

We generally assume that sin is extrovert, the cheerful and tipsy host, a crowd enjoying a shared malice. In truth, sin is lonely; it isolates us. Sin destroys relationship. Sinners are the people who know what they want, and they want only that. Notorious sinners are not lovers, husbands, mothers or friends (or at least, they are very bad lovers and friends). C. S. Lewis nailed that particular vice in *The Screwtape Letters* when he described the woman who is forever turning down the first offer of hospitality:

> She is always turning from what has been offered her to say with a demure little sigh and a smile 'Oh please, please . . . *all* I want is a cup of tea, weak but not too weak, and the teeniest weeniest bit of really crisp toast'.[4]

Her sin is gluttony (which is the sin that has a problem with appetite, and interestingly may well not insist on *too much* food). Sin turns her into impossible company. That is the key point. Sin does not just harm us, it disrupts community. That is why the early Church insisted that repentance must be public. Sinners have to find their way back into society.

Ash Wednesday, then, should not be focused on beginning Lent, or on declarations of intent – fewer chocolate hobnobs and more prayers. Ash Wednesday should be focused on repentance. It invites us to think again about our desire and the constant temptations that will diminish and isolate us. Ash Wednesday also asks us to accept the idea that people who repent can be forgiven. Like sin, forgiveness is a more difficult idea than we sometimes admit.

Forgiveness is a big idea. We should remember that one of the criticisms directed against Jesus, one of the things that made him offensive, was that he claimed to forgive sins.

> When Jesus saw their faith, he said to the paralytic, 'Take heart, son; your sins are forgiven.' Then some of the scribes said to themselves, 'This man is blaspheming.' (Matthew 9.2–3)

The objection to Jesus forgiving sins was, of course, that God alone can forgive. There was, though, another problem for Jesus' critics. His ministry was notable for the number of occasions on which he sat down with outcasts and sinners. Again and again, he included those people others were determined to keep out. We have already noticed how the Church identified and isolated sinners. That was done, in part, to acknowledge the seriousness of sin, the public damage it does. It was also done because boundaries make us feel safe; anxious communities like to build walls. Bringing in the outcast (or the migrant) generates a threat. Forgiving the person we have chosen to condemn, or even despise, is equally unsettling. In the story of the woman taken in adultery, we get a glimpse of the urgency and enthusiasm we have for identifying an outcast and the hypocrisy that sustains it. We feel better when we are clear that we belong, and we belong so profoundly when we have identified that it is 'us' against 'them'. Forgiveness demands that we give up on that kind of tribalism and include those people we have chosen to ignore. That is hard. As Rowan Williams has argued:

the person who forgives has renounced the safety of being locked into the position of the offended victim; he has decided to take the risk of creating afresh a relationship known to be dangerous, known to be capable of causing hurt.[5]

In fact, forgiveness requires both parties to surrender status. To repent is to abandon one set of certainties. We have all met (and some of us have been) the person who begins to inhabit and defend the idea that they are unacceptable, a failure, hopeless. Rather than apologize, or contemplate rebuilding what has been thrown down, it can feel easier to invest in despair. As Quentin Crisp explained, 'If at first you don't succeed, failure may be your style.' It can be very hard indeed to persuade someone who has thrown up walls of despair to give up on that identity and start again. Repentance makes us new, and to forgive is to commit, just as radically, to things being different. Those who have given offence and those who are offended routinely withdraw from one another and they tell different stories about what has happened. In repenting and forgiving we give up on those narratives and surrender our determination to make something of ourselves in order to accept what we might become in God's grace. Repentance and forgiveness commits us to a new and shared account of who we are. There is danger and uncertainty for both in that.

So forgiveness is not an exercise of power, it is much too risky to be that. Rowan Williams continues:

We should rather think of those extraordinary words in the prophecy of Hosea (11.8–9) about the mercy of God: 'How can I give you up, O Ephraim? For I am God and not a mortal'. To forgive is to share in the *helplessness* of God, who cannot turn from God's own nature.[6]

It is God's nature to forgive; God is powerless to do anything else. To repent and be forgiven is to recognize and embrace God's nature. It is far more than a judicial act. Forgiveness plunges us into new relationship with God and one another.

48

The Church is the communion of the forgiven. It is why, in the Lord's Prayer, we pray that we forgive one another. So, on Ash Wednesday and in the season that follows we say something radical and disturbing. We are marked with ash to help us die to what we are. We repent, we are washed, we change. We face in a different direction and we do that together; we face one another. The forgiveness that effects the change in us is a gift.

To hear us talk about Lent, giving things up, reading a Lent book, attending a Lent course, you would think this is the season of good works. We have it the wrong way round. Suppose I really want to be slim and admired (and suppose we overlook the fact that I have left it a bit late). I could stop eating quite so much cheese; I could buy shorts and run up hills (this *is* hypothetical). I could make myself slim. I could do that, but I cannot make myself admired. Admiration has to be given. In just the same way, in Lent we can learn to be penitent. Being sorry is a discipline; you can practise and improve. Indeed, we need to work at it because it is actually quite hard to be properly sorry. We know how to offer a qualified sorrow, as in, 'I am sorry you were upset when I shouted at you.' We can be extravagantly and meaninglessly sorry, as in, 'I know I shouted at you. I am useless and a worm and you must never speak to me again.' Being properly and precisely sorry, however, is much more difficult. I can work at that. When it comes to forgiveness, though, that has to be given. I can only be forgiven by you and by God. I cannot make it happen.

Forgiveness is a gift and it is always honest. It is a gift to the sinful, trapped in deceit, desperately determined to earn what can only be given.

Notes

1 Aelfric, *Lives of Saints*, ed. W. W. Skeat (London, 1881), I, p. 263.

2 T. Radcliffe, *Why Go to Church?* (London: Continuum, 2008), p. 18.

3 P. H. Pfatteicher, *Journey into the Heart of God: Living the Liturgical Year* (Oxford: Oxford University Press, 2013), p. 142.

4 C. S. Lewis, *The Screwtape Letters* (London: William Collins, 2016), pp. 87–8.

5 R. Williams, *Being Disciples: Essentials of the Christian Life* (London: SPCK, 2016), p. 40.

6 Williams, *Being Disciples*, p. 42.

6

Annunciation
Ordinary and extraordinary

There is a hymn that can be sung at the Feast of the Annunciation. It is number 161 in the *New English Hymnal*, 'For Mary, Mother of the Lord'. It is by J. R. Peacey (he was a canon of the cathedral in which I now work, although he died in 1971) and it describes the annunciation, Gabriel, and his message for Mary.

> For Mary, Mother of the Lord
> God's holy name be praised,
> Who first the Son of God adored
> As on her child she gazed.

At the end of the hymn, you will find a symbol against the author's name telling you that there has been what the editors call 'extensive alteration'. The change comes in verse two and you may perhaps need a degree in doctrine to make sense of what is going on. Peacey put Mary at the front and centre of his hymn:

> Brave, holy Virgin, she believed,
> though hard the task assigned,
> and by the Holy Ghost conceived
> the Saviour of Mankind.

Revising the hymn, editors shifted the emphasis.

> The angel Gabriel brought the word
> She should Christ's mother be;

Our Lady, handmaid of the Lord,
Made answer willingly.

It is not poetry that is changing here, it is faith. Mary herself becomes the victim of some theological jiggery-pokery.

The idea the editors were working with (and it is a perfectly respectable idea) is that salvation is the gift of God and that God alone is the agent. Peacey's first version of the hymn, calling her 'brave' and 'holy' and stressing the fact that she believed, gives her some agency. The later version of the hymn changes things: she is told what will happen. The difficulty here is the emphasis Peacey put on Mary. It could be thought that Mary won redemption for us, that she is a saviour of sorts. The editors of the *New English Hymnal* knew perfectly well that some Anglicans would not want to sing about Mary *saving* us.

There is always, in the Church of England, an awkwardness about Mary and what we say about her. It is an awkwardness that surfaces at the Feast of the Annunciation. She gets rewritten; her virginity and her status are debated. Part of the reason for the difficulty lies in old arguments and the desire to sound more, or less, like a Catholic. There is also, though, a conversation about the unique identity of Mary and the difficulty of describing her. There are two things to say about Mary and they sound contradictory. We need to say that she was extraordinary and then we need to say that she wasn't.

The annunciation was, without question, extraordinary. There is no debate about that. In the annunciation, heaven and earth touch one another. The word takes flesh. Indeed, the annunciation is so extraordinary that it gets stranded in its own holiness. Poets and artists lift the moment up so that we can admire it and then leave it lifted up. Mary and Gabriel drift away from time and place, on a current of grace. In paintings, they seem to live forever elegantly disposed on the edge of a garden. Edwin Muir, in his poem 'The Annunciation', plunges the angel and Mary into a 'trance'.

In the fresco of the annunciation painted by Fra Angelico for a cell in his own convent, the image is pared right down so that the figures appear to be isolated and utterly still.

It is all very beautiful and beguiling, but a bit misleading. The annunciation really must not have us looking into heaven. The focus is all the other way. The annunciation is set firmly in *this* world. Mary's spirituality may command our attention, but it is the physical reality that matters, and it sets the clock ticking. When St Luke tells the story (Luke is the only Gospel that describes the annunciation) he wants us to notice these things.

> In the sixth month the angel Gabriel was sent by God to a town in Galilee called Nazareth. (Luke 1.26)

'In the sixth month . . . in Galilee'; there is the stress on time and place. St Luke *keeps* giving us time and place. It is where he starts his Gospel, with Roman and Jewish history, Jerusalem, Nazareth and Bethlehem. Luke is determined that we will treat this as *history*. Luke knows the annunciation is an event, with a past and a future. St Paul makes the same point:

> when the fullness of time had come, God sent his Son, born of a woman, born under the law, in order to redeem those who were under the law, so that we might receive adoption as children. (Galatians 4.4–5)

The *fullness of time*: there is backstory to the annunciation, and it matters. Before we meet Gabriel, we have already met Elizabeth, who is 'getting on in years' and who has, remarkably, just become pregnant. We have heard her cry of vindication: 'This is what the Lord has done for me when he looked favourably on me and took away the disgrace I have endured among my people' (Luke 1.25). Those words are not entirely her own. She is quoting Rachel, who said just the same thing when she finally conceived and bore a child: 'God has taken away my reproach' (Genesis 30.23). All of this is deliberate. We are being reminded of the story of the patriarchs, of Abraham, Sarah,

Isaac, Rebekah, Jacob and Rachel, and all those moments when the promise that they would become a great nation nearly failed because children were not being born. When we meet Mary in Nazareth, in the sixth month, we are supposed to keep Genesis in mind and make these connections. History and prophecy were leading to this point. Mary is indeed part of the purposes of God.

The moment is extraordinary and Mary is extraordinary. There is a wonderful moment in the Orthodox liturgy in which it is not Mary who is fearful when the annunciation takes place, but Gabriel:

> Let creation rejoice and nature exult
> For the Archangel stands in fear before the Virgin.[1]

Mary says, 'Yes'. She does not succumb to fear, or temptation, she does not bargain, or beg. She simply says, 'Yes'. Here is someone who embraces the future (soon she will do that literally). She is courageous, not cynical, and she accepts God's will. When the word takes flesh, when Christ comes to us, everything turns on *obedience*. Christ does not stride in and seize humanity, he arrives dependent; he must be conceived. God does not overpower humanity, his messenger comes to Mary and she meets him with assent. That hymn with which we began this chapter employs an old and familiar idea in claiming that Mary is a *second Eve*. The sin of Eve in Eden was disobedience. Commanded that she could eat of any tree except the one in the midst of the garden, Eve took what she was told not to take. In the words of a fourteenth-century carol:

> All this world was forlorn,
> *Eva peccatrice*, (because of Eve's sin)
> Till our Lord was y-born
> *De te genitrice*, (of thee mother)
> with *ave* it went away,
> Darkest night, and comes the day
> *Salutis*: (salvation)
> The well springeth out of thee
> *Virtutis* (virtue)

Mary's obedience alters the flow of events. What *was* now gives way to what *will be*. Mary's great song of praise, which follows, can sound a bit measured and well mannered when it is sung at evensong, but it is radical stuff. Pride put down; might and wealth overturned. It is brave, valiant and stirring. Mary *is* extra-ordinary. The annunciation changes things and her 'Yes' is a trumpet call, a herald to a different future.

Make Mary *utterly* extraordinary, however, and you put her on a plinth, safely at a distance. We do have a tendency to suggest that holiness is something that only remarkable people can do. We turn them into statues to be sure that they will not do it any more. We create a holiness we cannot inhabit ourselves; we can admire Mary, but she ceases to be like us, she is no longer *family*. Good Protestants, meanwhile, will tell us that an extraordinary Mary elbows Jesus out of the way. They will rewrite hymns so that we do not get confused about who really makes the difference to our salvation. Make Mary too extraordinary and we get into trouble. So, the other thing we must say about Mary is that she is human. Mary is like us, one of us. She says 'Yes' and so can we. We do not have to be extraordinary; we just have to be human, like Mary. In her, quite literally *in her*, our humanity and God's divinity meet. It happens in her and it can happen in us. Holiness is not beyond our humanity.

Mary's holiness and the significance of the annunciation are rooted in obedience. If your model for human fulfilment is achieving your goals, living the dream or doing it 'my' way, then it would actually be Eve who looks more familiar. Mary's great achievement was to conform herself to the will of God, to see her future in the way that God saw it.

Note

1 Quoted in E. Behr-Sigel, *The Ministry of Women in the Church* (Crestwood, NY: St Vladimir's Seminary Press, 1991), p. 191.

7

Palm Sunday
Winners and losers

In *The Man Born to be King*, a radio play by Dorothy L. Sayers, Pilate dreams that God has died:

> And I asked . . . how could God die? And he answered 'don't you remember? They crucified him; he suffered under Pontius Pilate . . . Then all the people turned their faces to me and said Pontius Pilate [and they say it in Greek and Latin, in English, French and German] Pontius Pilate . . . Pontius Pilate . . . suffered under Pontius Pilate.[1]

Like a great top spinning on a needle tip, our salvation rests on one time and one place. It happened at Golgotha. When we tell that great story, we name a name. It happened, the creed tells us, 'under Pontius Pilate'. That name clamps the great purposes of God into the pages of our history books. That awful vision, of being named whenever the terrible crime is recalled, has come horrifyingly true. And it is not just in the creed. Demoniacs used to have the devil driven out of them in the name of Jesus Christ *who suffered under Pontius Pilate*. Converts were plunged into the baptismal waters, three times, and the name was spoken again and again, Jesus Christ who *suffered under Pontius Pilate*.

We know, our liturgy reminds us, and the Gospels insist, that our faith is rooted in history. Salvation has a time and place; it happened *under Pontius Pilate*. It is a truth we have already encountered in the celebration of Christmas when Luke insists on telling us that this happened when Augustus was emperor (Luke is particularly keen on these details and gives Pilate a mention at the beginning of Jesus' ministry). Christian faith rests on the life and death of Jesus. It is a summons into life and death, not away from it. It is flesh and bone, it is living and dying here, in this place and among these people. The great temptation, the one the monks of the desert feared, is the conviction that if only we could be somewhere else and start afresh we could be holy. Christian faith is history, not mystery.

That is not the same thing as saying that Christian faith *explains* history. When I began to study theology, in the 1970s, I was surrounded by uncertainties. My contemporaries and I, in our flares and our wide lapels, were the children of holocaust and nuclear war. We did not read headlines that gave us reassurance about the future, nor did we have much sense that we were making progress. We were also the grateful heirs of textual criticism. Academic study was all 'on the one hand', and 'on the other'. We thought that meaning was elusive and that you should hesitate before you insisted on some great narrative plan. We were not allowed to read the Hebrew Scriptures through the lens of the New Testament, assuming every prophecy was really about Jesus. So, we never thought that history was taking us somewhere and never assumed there was a grand plan. I am now genuinely surprised to look around, a generation later, and notice more and more Christians speak with mounting confidence about 'God's plan'.

Just before he took the oath of office at the inauguration ceremony in 2017, Donald Trump went to St John's Episcopal Church and heard a sermon. The preacher, Robert Jeffress, said:

President-elect Trump, I remember that it was exactly one year ago this weekend that I was with you on your Citation jet flying around Iowa before the first caucus or primary vote was cast. After our Wendy's cheeseburgers, I said that I believed that you would be the next President of the United States. And if that happened, it would be because God had placed you there. As the prophet Daniel said, it is God who removes and establishes leaders.[2]

It is all too easy (amid all that brand identity) to assume that a faith that talks about the providence of God or about prophecy is telling us that if you just pay proper attention you will see that history has a clear plan and that history is *going somewhere.*

To read the prophets is to discover that they believed nothing of the sort. You do not have to dig deep; the prophets so often wrote not out of confidence but in extravagant grief.

> I looked on the earth, and lo, it was waste and void; and to the heavens, and they had no light . . . I looked, and lo, the fruitful land was a desert, and all its cities were laid in ruins before the LORD, before his fierce anger. (Jeremiah 4.23, 26)

Jeremiah's anguish comes from frustrated purpose. Jeremiah was a Jewish theologian; it was a given for him that God creates. Yet that creative goodness was dissipated, and all that should be trusted was void. Creation had failed. Genesis was in reverse.

> Is there no balm in Gilead? Is there no physician there? Why then has the health of my poor people not been restored? O that my head were a spring of water, and my eyes a fountain of tears, so that I might weep day and night for the slain of my poor people! (Jeremiah 8.22 – 9.1)

There is no reassurance, no answer to the question, 'Is there no balm in Gilead?' Jeremiah weeps and goes on weeping. There is a popular misconception that the prophets took a kind of delight in disaster, a crazy pleasure in denunciation. In truth, there was no pleasure to be had: the sense of loss was bitter, absolute. Good historians will find continuity in a sequence of events, but they will also notice that some narratives are more difficult to plot, there are false starts, wrong turnings, sudden disasters. Theologians too know that faith does not suddenly provide a map to steer us through history. Jesus did not direct events on the black day on Golgotha; he refused to do that. *He suffered under Pontius Pilate.*

Week by week, Christians say the creed and bump into their own history, they hear the name of Pontius Pilate. On Palm Sunday, though, we attend to him more closely, for he is the defining figure in the Passion story that we read that day. We need this focus on Pilate and on Christ, who *suffered* on the cross, because Palm Sunday asks us to reflect on our history and to decide who Jesus really is.

We have observed Palm Sunday for a long time, but we have not done it consistently. Towards the end of the fourth century, a pilgrim called Egeria described the afternoon of Palm Sunday in Jerusalem. She spent three hours in a liturgy on the Mount of Olives and then went to a church for another service. Clearly, Egeria was a woman of piety and stamina: as that service ended she listened to St Matthew's account of Christ's entry into Jerusalem and then joined a procession into the city. The people carried branches and shouted, 'Blessed is he that cometh in the name of the Lord'. So, all those years ago, she was part of a Palm Sunday procession. The practice spread, but in 1548 the carrying of palms was abolished, on a tide of Protestant disapproval. As a consequence, you will not find Palm Sunday in the *Book of Common Prayer*; there it is simply the 'Sunday Next Before Easter'. The long gospel of the Passion was, however, retained. That is the constant on Palm Sunday.

Now, Palm Sunday processions are back. We notice the palms, and we probably pay even more attention to the donkey at the head of the procession, who (having done it before) knows the way and probably knows too all the words to 'Ride on, ride on in majesty'. Splendid as those things are, we should not allow ourselves to be distracted. The spotlight is on the cross. The collect for the day has always insisted on that. In Cranmer's mild revision of a very ancient text, in the *Book of Common Prayer* of 1549, the prayer begins:

Almighty and everlasting God, which, of thy tender love toward man, hath sent our Saviour Jesus Christ, to take upon him our flesh, and to suffer death upon the cross . . .

Palm Sunday sets before us the suffering of Christ. Our cheerful procession, with palms, leads us to the cross. So it should: everything leads to the cross, everything points to the suffering of Christ. Reading St John's Gospel there is a drumbeat insistence that there is a significant moment looming, an *hour* that will define everything. We hear it first at Cana:

The mother of Jesus said to him, 'They have no wine.' And Jesus said to her, 'Woman, what concern is that to you and to me? My hour has not yet come.' (John 2.3–4)

Then, with a startling frequency we hear Jesus tell others, the woman at the well or 'the Jews', that 'the hour is coming'. We are also told that Jesus cannot be arrested because 'his hour had not yet come'. All that changes as soon as the crowd seize palm branches and shout 'Hosanna'. Now, Jesus says,

The hour has come for the Son of Man to be glorified. (John 12.23)

This is the tipping point of the Gospel. Jesus, who has so relentlessly driven the pace of the narrative and been so active, suddenly becomes passive. Jesus did things; now things are done to him. There is a conversation with Pilate, and it tells us three times that Jesus has been 'handed over'. As Jesus comes to 'his hour', John insists that he is no longer in control.

And what should I say – 'Father, save me from this hour'? No, it is for this reason that I have come to this hour. (John 12.27)

John demands that we focus on this hour. It is an hour that only begins with palm branches; it is characterized by suffering.

Thirty-five years ago, the Anglican priest W. H. (Bill) Vanstone wrote a book called *The Stature of Waiting*. Vanstone was the kind of theologian who loved ancient languages and the meaning of words. His little book explains that while we are used to thinking that what Judas did was to *betray* Christ, what the Scriptures actually say is that he 'handed him over'. Vanstone also tells us that we routinely assume that the word *suffering* means being in pain and distress. In fact, earlier generations understood it differently. They thought that if you *suffered many things* that simply meant that a lot had happened to you. The point about the Passion, Vanstone argued, is that Jesus had to suffer it in the sense that it was *done to* him.

> It is not that He passes from success to failure, from gain to loss or from pleasure to pain: it is that He passes from doing to receiving what others do, from working to waiting, from the role of subject to the role of object and, in the proper sense of the phrase, from action to passion.[3]

Palm Sunday brings us to the moment when Jesus comes to this *hour*, the hour of passion, being *done to*. In Mark's Gospel, where there is a stark insistence on the fact that Jesus has been abandoned and where the suffering is unrelieved by any action he takes (no conversation with a penitent thief or with a beloved disciple), we are confronted by the fact that Jesus is passive, not active.

We live in a world of competition. We see it as a virtue to be in control. We talk a lot about 'exercising leadership'. It is important to us that we compete and win. In the USA, as I write this, Mr Trump has made the language of winning a necessary discourse. On the campaign trail he said, 'You gonna win so much you may even get tired of winning.' Even remarks about character and attitude became competitive: 'No one has more respect for women than I do,' or, 'I am the least racist person.' Everything is a competition. You do not have to look very deep into the internet to find such helpful items as *An Introvert's Guide to Winning in Love*, or an article on how to raise a 'winning child'. We are wired to compete; we live in rivalry, we have to impose ourselves. Jesus, however, refused to play that game. Jesus lived without rivalry or envy. That is why he had to suffer.

At the point of crisis in his ministry, when his hour had come, Christ was tempted to take control of the situation, tempted to impose himself and to make his own will and his own wishes his map and compass. He resisted that temptation: 'Nevertheless, not my will, but your will be done.' When he was brought before Pilate we should notice that Pilate debated power and authority; he wanted to know what power Christ had. Christ would not compete. He was indeed the King that Pilate looked for, but he made no claim, no boast.

Christ gave glory to God, and salvation to us, by resolutely refusing to make the most of himself. He gave himself up to his captors, he gave his spirit up to God upon the cross. He showed us that being fully human is not the same thing as clinging on to life, or status, or ambition. Jesus was King, he had authority, he taught as 'one with authority', but he did not have the kind of power that fascinated Pilate, and did not want it.

Christ showed us what it is to be fully alive and we could not bear to look. He lived and loved with an intensity we cannot bear and which we rejected. As the Dominican friar Herbert McCabe used to point out:

If you do not love, you will not be alive . . . If you do love you will be killed.[4]

Picking up our palms, palms that in countless pictures and church windows are the symbols of the sufferings and victories of the saints, we walk with Christ towards his cross. One of the best of all the Palm Sunday hymns was written by Samuel Crossman. Coincidentally he was, like me, Dean of Bristol. I can't quite follow him when he writes 'cheerful he to suffering goes'. There was nothing 'cheerful' about Gethsemane or the carrying of the cross. Crossman was right, however, when he wrote:

Never was love, dear King,
Never was grief like Thine.[5]

Christ lived our life fully. He showed us what it is to be fully human. A life that insists on its own way, that is focused on winning, is a life lived over and against others, a life lived in competition. It is isolation, not community. Similarly, the person who has to apologize at every turn, who cannot tell the truth for fear of giving offence, lives in a different kind of fear of relationship. Jesus lived in full humanity because he could live fully with others. To live fully, to live together, we have to give up our ambition and our obsession with power. Not just the fascination a few have for the butch and bruising forms of power, but the sly, beguiling kinds of power: the moral advantage, the intellectual edge, the wounded look, the over-extravagant apology, even the writhing determination to let others make the decisions. We have to give up all of it. Truth and grace do not barter.

Our Palm Sunday procession, our Palm Sunday gospel and the hosannas we sing recreate the way of the cross. They invite us to make a journey into a different kind of humanity and it is filled with risk.

Notes

1 D. L. Sayers, *The Man Born to be King* (Grand Rapids, MI: Eerdmans, 1943). First broadcast on 21 December 1941.

2 Sermon by Robert Jeffress on 20 January 2017 at St John's Episcopal Church, Washington DC, available at http://time.com/4641208/donald-trump-robert-jeffress-st-john-episcopal-inauguration/ (accessed 4 March 2019).

3 W. H. Vanstone, *The Stature of Waiting* (London: Darton, Longman & Todd, 1982), p. 31.

4 H. McCabe, *God Matters* (New York: Continuum, 1987), p. 218.

5 Samuel Crossman, 'My song is love unknown'.

8

Good Friday
Not waving, not drowning

Facing the cross

In one of the medieval passion plays, the centurion provides a commentary as the nails are hammered home. 'Flesh' at the first blow; then, 'bone' as he hears the second; and finally, 'wood'. Crucifixion was a very physical thing. Christ wins redemption bitterly, from hard, unyielding things. He wrestles salvation from unwilling flesh, bone and wood. We need to notice that. There is an old temptation that wants us to turn faith into spirituality. When C. S. Lewis imagined the ways devils might tempt us, he had his wily old devil, Screwtape, say, 'Keep his mind on the inner life.'

> It is, no doubt, impossible to prevent his praying for his mother, but we have means of rendering the prayers innocuous. Make sure they are always very 'spiritual', that he is always concerned with the state of her soul and never with her rheumatism . . . he will in some degree be praying for an imaginary person daily less and less like the real mother – the sharp-tongued old lady at the breakfast table.[1]

Good Friday, like Christmas and Easter, demands that we talk about bodies. Salvation is worked out in our lives, not in our minds. What happens to Christ on the cross, his agony, his death and burial, are not distractions from the business of faith, they are literally 'crucial'.

So, it is essential that we come to the cross and face it squarely, in all its horror. That is a point that St John insists upon. He talks about Jesus being 'lifted up', Jesus being *shown* to us so that he might 'draw all people to myself' (John 12.32). We are supposed to look at this. What is it we are supposed to see? The answer is straightforward; it is obvious. We are supposed to see a man dying. One of the earliest works of literature in English is a story, in verse, told as if the cross of Christ could speak. *The Dream of the Rood* wants us to see what happened to Christ: 'On me the only Begotten, the Son of God suffered.'

> I saw the Lord of Hosts
> Outstretched in agony.[2]

We should pay attention to the agony, the dying, the death. We would rather not do that. We flinch and look away. There is another, equally splendid poem, written years after the *Dream of the Rood* by John Donne. It is called 'Good Friday, 1613. Riding Westward'. Donne cannot see the cross (he is thinking *east*, but he is travelling *west*); he is facing the wrong way.

> Yet dare I almost be glad, I do not see
> That spectacle of too much weight for me.

Donne is making a theological point; the cross is overwhelming. In one sense, it is hard to look at the cross because there is just so much to see, it beggars the imagination. It is also, however, a moral point. It is hard to look at the cross because it is repellent. We do not look for meaning in suffering. We see pain in simply negative terms; it is something to be borne and *got over*, an interruption before life can resume a proper course. Which is why, of course, we have inherited a dreadful vocabulary about the *disabled*, *deformed* and *incapacitated*. There is a long tradition that turned away from the cross; pagans found images of the cross baffling or depraved. Meanwhile, one of the earliest Christian heretics suggested that Jesus, the glorious Son of God, was not brought so low and only *appeared* to suffer on the cross.

St John was right; the cross is where Jesus is *lifted up*. Unless we look and see him suffer and die we will never understand the incarnation. Jesus becomes like us in life *and* in death. Even suffering, dying and death are gathered into God. They are sanctified, they are redeemed, they too are places of encounter with God. Of all the things we have to say about the cross, this perhaps is the most neglected. As we rush on to explain what the cross means, we fail to see it as the most radical statement of incarnation. God is with us in life and with us in death: 'Jesus . . . born in human likeness . . . and . . . obedient to the point of death – even death on a cross' (Philippians 2.5, 7–8). Suffering and death will still challenge us, still bring us to breaking point, but we do not have to describe them as inter-ruptions in the real business of living. Rather we must insist that here too we find God.

The cross, and Christ upon it, the radical and absolute encounter of the life of God and human dying, is indeed some-thing that needs to be seen. There will always be more to say. 'Everything dependeth upon the Cross', said Thomas à Kempis:

> there is none other way unto life and to true inward peace, except the way of the Holy Cross and of daily mortification. Go where thou wilt, seek whatsoever thou wilt, and thou shalt find no higher way above nor safer way below, than the way of the Holy Cross.[3]

In the hands of Thomas à Kempis the cross becomes a direc-tion of travel; it defines Christian faith. For Paul it is the power of God, and a way of making peace (1 Corinthians 1.18; Colossians 1.20). Christ's death on the cross reconciled us to God (Romans 5.10) and his blood was an atonement (Romans 3.5). Everything we have to say about faith, about God and about ourselves is here. The Christian year culminates here and the new creation begins at Easter. All our richest (and by the same token our most complex) ideas about faith find expres-sion here: justification, redemption, atonement . . . No one account of the cross can capture that range of meaning. No one description of what Christ did upon the cross contains all its meaning. As Rowan Williams explains:

> The meaning of the cross of Jesus is something that constantly moves between different poles. The deeper you go into any one meaning, any one metaphor, the more it seems you're likely to bump into another one. You can't fully talk about the sign without the victory, the victory without the sacrifice. And that's as it should be. Christian theology is not a set of granite monuments that you walk around with your guidebook, ticking them off one by one . . .[4]

No surprise then that John Donne might be grateful for turning away on Good Friday. The cross is a dread-full thing to contemplate and the ideas are overwhelming.

Confronted with such richness (and complexity), Good Friday invites us to hear the story of Christ's Passion. Hear the story, see the cross. It is important to stay with the story. The preaching and liturgy on Good Friday is the longest in the year, and we are invited to stay with it. That is not our first instinct. I have already suggested that we turn away from suffering; we look elsewhere for meaning and explanation. One of the things we should notice in the long hours of the Passion is that Christ says so little, offers no explanation. In John's Gospel there is a brief exchange with the beloved disciple and Mary that has Christ building the Church out of his death. In Luke there is a meditation on forgiveness that gathers in the penitent thief. That is little enough. In Mark and Matthew there is a staggering silence. Jesus endures the cross; he does not explain it, or make sense of it.

Looking for a different outcome

Looking away from the cross, looking elsewhere, there is a temptation to want some better or different outcome. The crowd at the foot of the cross wondered if Elijah would come to save Jesus. The priests mocked Jesus for his determination to save others and his inability to save himself. Pilate wondered about a political outcome, the kind of a solution a king might impose. At the foot of the cross the speculation was all about a religious solution. As Christ was condemned and dying those around him debated what power might do in these circumstances. Christ, meanwhile, suffered and died. Believing in Christ, following Christ, means accepting that God is precisely in the midst of life, even in suffering and death. God is not out there somewhere ready to intervene suddenly and trump this experience, turn it into something else. What Good Friday tells us is that this life is not a kind of fiction because real life is actually somewhere else ready to let loose a champion on a charger to come and save us. It is not an easy lesson to learn, but Good Friday assures us that the good news of the gospel is that our lives and even our deaths are reality. There is no other story.

Finding that hard to accept, we try to shift responsibility, create a different story. One of the striking things about the Good Friday story is the stress on Christ's innocence. Pilate interrogates Jesus and then goes out to the Jews saying, 'I find no case against him' (John 18.38). Pilate finds Christ innocent, but *still*, he condemns him. It is not just that Christ is innocent of insurrection and blasphemy, the charges that are laid against him. He is innocent of the sins that so utterly compromise the rest of us: the fear that makes us too cautious, the ambition that makes us too eager. Christ is blameless, and remember, Christ does not seek this death. In Gethsemane he prays that he might avoid it.

For Pilate, for the religious authorities and for the crowd the cross is pointless. It is not justice. Christ is innocent; this death will achieve and prove nothing. Christ is innocent; we, meanwhile, are preoccupied with blame. There is a lot of recrimination and blame in the story of the cross. Famously, the Gospels blame the Jews. So, John tells us that Pilate wanted to release Jesus, but the Jews cried out against him. In Matthew, chillingly, we hear Jews say, 'His blood be on us and on our children!' (Matthew 27.25). There is more than a whiff of anti-Semitism here. The desire to point the finger of blame is ironic. Christ goes to the cross, he bears the blame and *still* we insist on blaming one another. It is seductive, this business of blame. If the government is to blame for reducing access to benefits, then the beggars in the street are the government's problem, not mine. If my friend chooses to sulk then it is her fault and her problem. More subtle, and if anything more dangerous, if it is *entirely* my fault that I have upset you, then I am just a failure and there is nothing to be done. Blame drives us into blind alleys where we never need engage with others. In a culture of blame there is no company to be had.

The business of blame and responsibility, the shouting crowd, Pilate washing his hands, the urgent message from his wife, 'have nothing to do with this man', is part of the temptation to look away from the cross, to see the story, the actors somewhere else. We look either for a rescue from off-stage that will tell us this was never really the story anyway, or for the agent, the perpetrator, of this tragedy, because then we have someone to *blame*. We would much rather do that than look at ourselves.

Our God has taken flesh and become a human being. He has not become any human being, just another Tom, Dick or Harriet. Jesus is *the* human being. He is what we are supposed to be. As Herbert McCabe put it, 'Jesus was the first human being who had no fear of love at all, the first to have no fear of being human.'[5] On Good Friday, the crowd that had gone wild with joy on Palm Sunday suddenly sees what that really means. This true humanity does not assert itself and produce an act of power, nor does it cut its losses and plead or blame. Jesus accepts that there is no other story. The crowd cannot bear what it sees. Pilate gives them a vote, so they can choose who should be released. Asked to vote for Christ's humanity, they baulk; they vote for the power and confidence of the bandit Barabbas. Christ does not die because the Jews, or Pilate, are to blame. Jesus dies because there is no other story we will accept.

This outcome was never in doubt. These scenes in Jerusalem are not an awkward appendix to the real story of Jesus' teaching and healing; *this* is the real story. From the beginning, Jesus was the Lamb of God, the one who would die. The whole story of the gospel is the story of the cross. As Lancelot Andrewes put it, 'In this all, so that, see this and see all . . .' He continues:

> It is well known that Christ and his cross were never parted, but that all his life long was a continual cross. At the very cratch (the crib), His cross first began. There Herod sought to do what Pilate did even to end his life before it began . . .[6]

The whole gospel is the cross (a point Thomas à Kempis also makes). It is important that we understand this. Turning to the cross, as we should, we have probed deeply into its mysteries. We have tried to explain the difference that the cross makes, what Christ achieved there. We have talked of his death as a 'sacrifice', or an 'atonement', or as 'paying the penalty of sin'. We understand it often as an offering he made to God on our behalf.

> There was no other good enough
> To pay the price of sin.
> He only could unlock the gate
> Of heav'n and let us in.[7]

As Rowan Williams explains, no single answer exhausts the meaning of the cross. We need all the language we have for a salvation that reaches all times and all places. On the cross, our refusal to accept our own humanity meets God's freedom to act. Our constraint encounters God's freedom. When constraint and freedom meet, no simple explanation will suffice. We will always need different ways of describing what happens on the cross.

The cross is the whole gospel. The cross sums up what we see in Christ's birth and ministry. As Eamon Duffy puts it, 'The death of Jesus is from beginning to end an offering. It is an offering not *to*, but *from* God.'[8] What we see on the cross is our own humanity and the life and love of God. This is what

God looks like when God lives among us. It turns so many assumptions inside out. The second-century bishop Melito of Sardis provided a list:

> The whole creation was amazed, marvelling and saying,
> 'What new mystery, then, is this?
> The Judge is judged, and holds his peace;
> The Invisible One is seen, and is not ashamed;
> The Incomprehensible is laid hold upon, and is not indignant;
> The Illimitable is circumscribed, and doth not resist;
> The Impassible suffereth, and doth not avenge;
> The Immortal dieth, and answereth not a word;
> The Celestial is laid in the grave, and endureth!
> What new mystery is this?'[9]

The cross is the whole gospel. The cross is the life of God as it is lived among us. The cross is what perfect humanity looks like. Jesus took flesh that we might be like him. Unfortunately, we keep trying to get the boot on the other foot; we want to make him become like us. We can see this desire working its way out in the things that are sometimes said about what happens to Jesus during his Passion. Harry Williams once argued, passionately, 'His experience as a human being was identical with our own.'[10] Williams wrote about Jesus' 'panic' and about the cry of dereliction from the cross, 'My God, my God, why have you forsaken me?' He argued that Jesus is most fully human, most perfectly human, precisely in that abandonment and (what Williams took to be) despair. Because our feelings of doubt and despair are the worst and strongest feelings that we have, we assume that these feelings are the real benchmark of our humanity. Doubt and despair become badges of pride. Then we insist that Jesus had those feelings too. We are mistaken. We are not most alive, not *fully* human, at the moments when we despair of humanity and forget how to hope. We are actually *less* than ourselves at moments like that. Jesus did not take flesh to be like us, he took flesh so that we might be like him. Jesus did not despair. When Jesus cried out on Golgotha he used words that come straight from his prayer book, from Psalm 22. He was praying.

There is no other story. Jesus does not become fully human as he dies. God does not rescue him. The suffering is pointless, it has to be endured, it is not explained.

Good Friday is the moment when Jesus is lifted up so that we can see him. We see his humanity. We see the life of God and he prays himself home.

Notes

1 C. S. Lewis, *The Screwtape Letters* (London: William Collins, 2016), p. 12.

2 *The Faber Book of Religious Verse*, ed. Helen Gardner (Faber and Faber, 1972), p. 26.

3 Thomas à Kempis, *The Imitation of Christ* II.xii.3 (London: Fontana, 1963), pp. 103–4.

4 R. Williams, *God With Us: The Meaning of the Cross and Resurrection Then and Now* (London: SPCK, 2017), p. 54.

5 H. McCabe, *God Matters* (London: Bloomsbury, 2010), p. 95.

6 L. Andrewes, 'Sermon III' in *Ninety-Six Sermons by Lancelot Andrewes*, Vol. 2 (Oxford, 1851), p. 166.

7 Cecil Frances Alexander, 'There is a green hill far away'.

8 E. Duffy, *The Creed in the Catechism: The Life of God For Us* (London: Geoffrey Chapman, 1996), p. 67.

9 'Ante-Nicene Fathers VIII' in A. Roberts and J. Donaldson (eds), *Ante-Nicene Fathers: The Writings of the Fathers Down to A.D. 325* (Peabody, MA: Hendrickson, 1999), p. 756.

10 H. Williams, *True Wilderness* (London: Mowbray Morehouse Publishing, 1994), p. 43.

9

Easter Eve
That was the end

Telling the truth

The first job I had after ordination was as a curate, in Cambridge. A friend ordained a few years earlier had started his ministry on a housing estate in Sheffield, living in a tower block. He spent the night before his ordination sheltering a female neighbour (a woman he had only just met) from a very angry man who was trying to beat down his front door. My curacy was also on a housing estate, but the drama was altogether less vivid. Quite early on, I was asked to visit an elderly couple who had just had some bad news from the doctor. Dorothy and Bill (not their real names) were struggling to adjust to the idea that she was terminally ill. It was a slow decline at the beginning and I visited many times over a number of months. While they tried to find the words for what was happening to them, I learnt about ministry to the dying. Between us, we had some successes, but some of what we said and did troubles me still. The conspiracies and silences around death are the problem. Clergy often find that they are in the business of giving permission: telling the very elderly, or the very sick, that it is not odd, or unacceptable, to say that they want to die. Families occasionally have to be persuaded to give up on the myth that the patient is going to get better. Everyone has to get used to the idea that death is now part of the story and must be named. In my early visits to Dorothy and Bill she would sometimes be in bed and he would be in the sitting room. I would encounter two different narratives. He would be worrying that he could not get her to eat and she would be a bit tetchy about the idea that she might want food. I helped them with that and soon they managed without my services as an interpreter.

More difficult was the conversation I had with Dorothy about dying. We got on well enough and she liked the fact that I never tried to change the subject. I was, though, far too slow to notice that my answers to her questions were too tentative. I gave her no confidence, no satisfaction. I could not tell her what would happen when she died. I could not describe heaven to her. She wanted more and I did not quite notice and did not have more to say. Then I went away for a week or two. When I next saw her, she was filled with an energy I had not seen for months. She had been visited by a distant relative who was pastor to a church in North America, I think possibly Canada. He had given her the answers she craved. He had told her she would have money in heaven, she would be rich, and that made all the difference. It had never occurred to me to tell her that, and honestly it is not something I would say now. There was no denying, though, that it helped her. She wanted a different ending.

For some, those who are in great pain or just exhausted, death can be welcome. For many of us, it is just frightening. It is frightening because it is unknown and it is frightening because it is the wrong ending. Even those of us who die well will die incomplete with things that have been left unsaid and unresolved. At death there is always potential that has not always been fulfilled; death catches us before the story has been fully concluded and properly told. Dorothy wanted a story that included the money that she had never had (though she was not by any measure poor). She wanted a part to play, spending power, a bit of control. Death steals the role we play, it ends the story we are acting out in our head. Another Dominican writer, Simon Tugwell, explains it like this:

> Death, although it ends a story in one sense, is an unsatisfactory ending. All too often it does not round off a life which

can be seen as complete, it just cuts it off brutally. And it is but the last in a whole series of meaningless frustrations.[1]

Tugwell is right; confronted by death we must say something about the 'wrongness' of it. There are good reasons why brave and thoughtful people might wish for death and welcome it. The fundamental insight of scripture, however, is that death is the wrong ending. It was in Genesis a punishment meted out to Adam and Eve. It is to Paul 'the last enemy' (1 Corinthians 15.26). Jesus himself weeps over the death of Lazarus. Death disrupts our story because it was never part of the story. It is an intruder, it is *fallen*, and it is wrong. Struggling with our own dying, we struggle too with Christ's death and what to say. We should notice that there is no liturgy for the death of Christ, no liturgy for Easter Eve. At points in our history we have hurried over this difficult day. Older Roman Catholic liturgies which took place on the morning of Easter Eve contracted the period in which Christ must be considered dead to a matter of hours. In the *Book of Common Prayer* there is a collect, epistle and gospel for Easter Eve. The collect (which is probably by John Cosin) is reluctant to rest in this particular moment. It chooses instead to look both backwards and forwards. As we were once baptized into Christ's death, it prays:

> so by continual mortifying our corrupt affections we may be buried with him; and that, through the grave, and gate of death, we may pass to our joyful resurrection.

In *Common Worship*, on Good Friday and Easter Eve all we have are Morning and Evening Prayer. Both those services are pared right down. Not only is the Gloria omitted, but opening and concluding prayers disappear, making the service feel odd and a little awkward. We feel the dislocation of death. On Easter Eve, churches are largely silent (well, that is the intention, though in my cathedral you are quite likely to bump into flower arrangers anticipating Easter and vergers bustling about with candles). Even so, the cathedral is stripped of colour and ornament and the lights are switched off. Like Cosin's collect, we seem to hesitate between the past and the future. A bare altar signals something of our loss. Christ's death is certainly not what we celebrate.

The wrong ending

Death is the wrong ending. In Christian theology it is thought of as the abiding impact of the Fall. It cannot be part of what we celebrate in the Christian story, but it must be acknowledged. We used to do that well. We used to set this truth before us. From the fourteenth century onwards the image of the dead Christ, known as the *Image of Pity*, was a focus of Christian devotion and reflection. Examples abound: there was a famous icon in the Basilica di Santa Croce in Gerusalemme, Rome, and endless images painted above altars, statues (think of Michelangelo's *Pietà*), and masterpieces like Holbein's dead Christ, or paintings of the deposition by (among others) Bellini, Dürer, Mantegna, Memling and van der Weyden. Seeing these, and cheap images that also began to circulate, there could be no doubt that the stark reality of Christ's death was taken to the heart of the faith.

They all knew, these artists, that death is real and that we have to come at Easter through Easter Eve. Christ died. He really was dead. It is one of the most ancient and persistent heresies of the Church that somehow this death was temporary or not quite *real*. Jesus died. His life was over. That story finished, in the words of the former Cambridge Professor of Divinity Nicholas Lash:

> Jesus' life ended on Good Friday afternoon, between two thieves. And that was the end.[2]

Not only did Jesus die, but his death was every bit as complete and final for him as it is for us. Although Christian teachers and certainly any number of heretics have struggled with the idea that Jesus died completely and absolutely, that is what we believe. So determined was the Church to make the point that early creeds quickly began to insist that Jesus died and went where all the dead go. We inherit that insistence in our own creed:

> I believe in Jesus Christ, his only Son, our Lord, who . . . was crucified, died, and was buried; he descended to the dead . . .

Jesus died.

When we go on to talk about Easter, we must understand that it is not the happy ending to the horrid business of Good Friday. Christians know death to be real. We do not say that Jesus was dead 'for a while' and then he came back to life. Jesus died on Good Friday. That is why the Gospels go to such trouble to tell us that the risen Christ had the marks of the nails. It was a dead body they saw. Jesus died and was dead. It is fundamentally important we understand this truth. Christian faith is not a sort of cosmic joke. We do not say that death only *seems* frightening. We do not believe that death is temporary. Death is the fearsome thing we know it to be. Death, desertion, betrayal, torture, injustice and all those other things visited on Jesus are evil and they remain evil. God does not murmur, 'there, there', at Easter and brush them all aside. Easter does not tell us that we can forget about death and treat it as irrelevant. Once we have understood that, once we have understood that Easter does not cancel out Good Friday, we can begin to think about what Easter does say about Good Friday.

Easter is not the happy ending to Good Friday. Easter is the *explanation* of Good Friday. Easter is the way you look at Good Friday. Jesus was betrayed, deserted, beaten, unjustly condemned, crucified and killed. God, in Christ, endured that, took it to himself. Even death is gathered into God. Death is not set aside, nor is it dismissed; death is redeemed. At Easter, everything that looked as though it was *just* an ending, *just* a failure, *just* a defeat begins to look like something else.

What began in his life has not finished in his death. Christ's death is still there, but now we see it differently. In Matthew's Gospel there is a tiny detail that helps us understand. Matthew is interested, indeed really interested, in what happens just before Easter. Matthew alone tells us that a guard is posted on Jesus' tomb. The chief priests demand that; they are worried that 'his disciples may go steal him away, and tell the people, "He has been raised from the dead" (Matthew 27.64). So, Matthew shows us that Jesus dies and armed force continues to hold sway. All those powers of denial and despair, with their muscle and steel, blocking hope. Then an angel appears with news of the resurrection and Matthew adds the telling detail:

> For fear of him the guards shook and became like dead men.
> (Matthew 28.4)

The armed force is still there, that brutality, that power to deny hope, and Jesus is still dead. It is a dead body his friends see. Yet both are changed. Now Jesus thrills with life and the soldiers seem dead. Death is real, but it is not what we thought it was and neither is life. Jesus is overcome and dies on Good Friday. At Easter, it is death that is overcome. That is the story we need to tell.

When I was a graduate student, my vicar was Michael Mayne. In those days, he was the vicar of the University Church in Cambridge and rather admired as a good preacher. Later, he had a distinguished ministry as Dean of Westminster and wrote a series of much acclaimed books. I could not say we were ever friends, but when I went on to ordination and returned to Cambridge as a college chaplain, I invited him to preach more than once, and got to know him better. Later still, in retirement, he began to write what he had decided would be his final book. It began not so very differently from other books he had written. Then, in the summer of 2005, he was diagnosed with cancer of the jaw. At that point, *The Enduring Melody* took a remarkable turn. As he examined what he thought about his own death, he wrote with an even greater frankness and power. Faith offered him no insurance; he worried that it might fail him, that he might fail this test. Then, as the end drew very near, he wrote this:

> We each choose to die in our own way, though for some it will be harder than for others . . . trying (however reluctantly, however painfully) to deliberately unseal our clenched fists and let go of what we have been given with open hands . . .[3]

I am not sure he made the connection, but it is telling that he wrote about death and thought about letting go. It is an echo of what Jesus said to Mary Magdalene in the garden:

> Do not hold on to me, because I have not yet ascended to the Father. (John 20.17)

You have to let go.

Jesus died. In John's Gospel his last words were, 'It is finished' (or, sometimes, 'It is accomplished') and then he 'bowed his head and gave up his spirit'. His death is an article of faith. Jesus gave up his spirit, or better still, the word translates as he 'handed it over'. *He* did this; it was not done to him, or for him. Augustine explains:

> Who can thus sleep when he pleases, as Jesus dies when He pleased? . . . Who is there that thus departs when he pleases, as He departed this life at his pleasure? How great the power to be hoped for or dreaded that must be His as judge, if such was the power He exhibited as a dying man.[4]

It is finished. Dying at his own command, he takes the act of dying and death itself into the life of God.

Most of us fear to die because we feel that we have something to lose. We worry that we will die incomplete with some part of our story not told. There will be things not said, not felt, there will be experiences we have missed. We do not feel that our lives are an accomplishment, or that they are complete.

Christ said, 'It is finished', and there was nothing that he wanted to keep. He had found his identity. His life was yielded up. He was handed over; he let go.

Think back to Eden and that first sin. It was a sin of possessiveness; Eve *took* the apple. Now Christ gives everything up. We struggle with this as we try so hard to be what we are and hope for more. Christ did not struggle at all, accepting rather what he would become. He did not take, he received. This is fundamental. God would give us the kingdom but only if we will have it in preference to what we have now. Life has been a gift and can be surrendered. To live, to really live, we must first let go.

Notes

1 S. Tugwell, *Human Immortality and the Redemption of Death* (Darton, Longman & Todd, 1990), p. 84.

2 N. Lash, *Seeing in the Dark: University Sermons* (London: Darton, Longman & Todd, 2005), p. 111.

3 M. Mayne, *The Enduring Melody* (London: Darton, Longman & Todd, 2006), p. 250.

4 Augustine, *On the Gospel of John* in P. Schaff (ed.), *Nicene and Post-Nicene Fathers VII* (Peabody, MA: Hendrickson, 1999), p. 434.

10

Easter
Not a new story,
but a better explanation

Have you believed because you have seen me?

The Church believes that every Sunday is an Easter day. Sunday is the first day of the week, the first day of a new creation. That new creation is constantly renewed. Every Sunday is Easter Day. The critical idea here is that we do not *keep* Easter, we do not *observe* Easter; rather, we live inside it. Christ's birth was an event, so was the crucifixion. Easter is not *an event*. Easter is a conviction, an attitude. Easter is not history; Easter is the future.

Commentators routinely and carefully remind us that the Easter stories in the Gospels are very different from one another. Different evangelists tell different stories. A locked room in Jerusalem, a lakeside in Galilee, a mountaintop, or a country road, we range widely as we read what the evangelists wrote. At Easter, it can seem as though the story runs away with us. We can no longer contain the narrative. Christ's risen life is let loose in the world and it becomes impossible to tell one single or simple story of what that looks like. The commentators are telling us something significant, but we should still notice that these different stories are actually remarkably similar. In their own way, each one makes the same point. In the garden early in the morning, or sitting in a boat in Galilee looking to the shore, or on the road to Emmaus, the same challenge is repeated and reprised. Who is this? Do you know him? At Easter, the only significant question is, 'Do you see?' It is St John who puts that question most forcefully. When Thomas finally does see, and makes the great confession of faith, 'My Lord and my God', Jesus replies:

> Have you believed because you have seen me? Blessed are those who have not seen and yet have come to believe. (John 20.29)

Years after my rather hapless first attempts to offer something to someone who was dying, I became a vicar in London. A rather occasional member of the congregation became ill with a very aggressive cancer. There was no time for long conversations spreading over weeks, trying out one idea and then another. I arrived at his door wondering how I would find words for a situation and a man I did not know particularly well. I need not have worried. The door was thrown open and he was in front of me, urging me to come in and to follow him. He had worked in a museum, he was a collector, and he had found something I simply had to look at. 'Come and see,' he said. Will you see? From the beginning of Jesus' ministry, this was the oppressing question. John's Gospel begins with the grand assertion that we have *seen* God's glory, 'the glory as of a father's only son' (John 1.14). There is a trumpet call from the start announcing that this is all about paying attention, being able to see. Then we encounter Jesus, and immediately we hear him invite the disciples to 'come and see' (John 1.39). Easter turns on a light so that we can see. It sets us in the presence of God's glory and drives away the shadows. In the words of the *Exultet*,

> Be glad, let earth be glad, as glory floods her,
> ablaze with light from her eternal King,
> let all corners of the earth be glad,
> knowing an end to gloom and darkness.

Easter is sight, light in dark places, a perspective; an explanation.

> Christ your Son,
> who, coming back from death's domain,

has shed his peaceful light on humanity,
and lives and reigns for ever and ever.[1]

Orthodox icons of the resurrection have Jesus trampling down broken doors. Around him are shattered locks and broken chains. It is a victory over constraint and it is shattering. Some Anglican hymns, by contrast, turn to nature for a much less alarming set of images (to suit a nation of gardeners):

> Christ the first fruits
> Of the holy harvest field[2]

Even in quiet shires or polite suburbs, however, the dislocation of Easter is never far away. This is a significant, even a violent shift in our understanding.

> Love's redeeming work is done,
> Fought the fight, the battle won.[3]

Easter sees it differently; Easter changes things. Easter is unique; it is not *like* anything else.

Cause and effect

As a schoolboy historian, I had to write essays that looked backwards and searched out patterns. I wrote about the *causes* of the English Civil War, the *origins* of the French Revolution. If I worked hard enough, consulted the right experts, got the facts right, then it was assumed I could explain why *this* led to *that*. You could find a direction of travel and history would add up, make sense. Or at least that was the theory I laboured with, as my essays got longer and more and more indigestible. Schoolboys who stick with the study of history, however, soon learn to be a little less confident. The awkwardness of the past keeps escaping; it refuses to be tamed. Historians have to learn humility.

Theologians must learn the lesson too. The Gospel stories of the resurrection do not give us lengthy explanations of what it all means. Pick up Mark's Gospel and one thing you will notice is that there is a curious hesitation about this extraordinary news. Mark tells us that Mary Magdalene, Mary the mother of James, and Salome came to the tomb where Jesus had been buried (Mark 16.1). There, they met a young man who frightened them. Even though this young man instructed them to go and tell the Disciples that Jesus was going ahead of them, they were not reassured:

> they went out and fled from the tomb, for terror and amazement had seized them; and they said nothing to anyone, for they were afraid. (Mark 16.8)

The witnesses of the resurrection certainly *see* something. They are often at a loss about what they should *say*.

Mark names the three women who went to the tomb. He wants to remind us that they were the ones who stood fast at the foot of the cross; still there when everyone else had run away. These three women did not see the resurrection; they could not describe the resurrection. What they *could* describe was the cross. We do need to notice that it is people who had seen Jesus die who first hear about the resurrection. It was important that they knew that he had truly died before they encountered his risen life. These women had the facts straight. They would never wonder if Jesus might just possibly have survived. They could not possibly think that he might have been taken down not quite dead. They knew what they had seen. They brought spices. They came looking for a dead body.

Accounts of the resurrection begin with the bald fact that Jesus was dead. Then they confront us with something else. They do not agree. In Matthew, there was an earthquake and an angel rolls away the stone. In Mark, the stone has already been moved and there is a young man sitting nearby. In Luke, there are two men. Different things are said. This is not a sequence of events. We must not rush in and arrange all the elements, neatly, into a pattern. This is not the last twist of the plot.

The great Christian truth is that God showed himself to us in the one way we might best understand – as a human being – and he died. What does God look like? He looks like Jesus on the cross. St John insists on that point; he reminds us that Jesus is best seen when he is 'lifted up' for us, on the cross. After the resurrection, he still looks like that man on the cross. We see the wounds. Jesus died. It is a hard idea to grasp, but Easter wants us to keep seeing the death, the wounds and the cross. That bit of the story is not over. Death is not a hiccup in a story that is actually about something else. In the resurrection death does not disappear. Jesus is dead and alive. In the words of an early liturgy, he 'lives slain'.

Easter is not the next bit of the narrative, as though it is simply a question of saying 'on Friday he died, on Sunday he was alive again'. Easter is not the last chapter in an autobiography, it is the commentary on all that has come before; it is the way we read the story and understand it. It is in the Emmaus story that we get a glimpse of what that means. Emmaus only figures in the Gospel of St Luke. He, of course, is the evangelist who keeps taking us to Jerusalem. The Gospel begins there, there is a long and strong narrative about Jesus journeying to Jerusalem and a clear sense of destiny:

> I must be on my way, because it is impossible for a prophet to be killed away from Jerusalem. (Luke 13.33)

No surprise, then, that at the end of the Gospel the Disciples return to Jerusalem 'with great joy'. Jerusalem is where they are supposed to be. All of which tells us that when Luke begins a story on the road to Emmaus he is making a very significant statement. He knows that these two travellers are going in the wrong direction. They are leaving Jerusalem, they have turned their backs on the cross and on everything they nearly, but not quite, understood. As they walk on, Jesus meets them (we should notice that the initiative lies with Jesus, he comes to find them). He joins in their conversation. He walks on with them, even though they continue to go in the wrong direction.

They do not know who it is: 'their eyes were kept from recognizing him'. That is reassuring. If we find the resurrection surprising, even baffling, we are in good company. There is plenty of evidence that the Disciples were equally wrong-footed, and some of them at least were very dubious. The resurrection was unlooked for; it remains astonishing. It is surprisingly easy to be blind to what has happened. The two disciples on the Emmaus road talk of events and what has happened; they review their experience all over again. The events have plunged them into despair. History has failed them; it has gone nowhere:

> Jesus of Nazareth, who was a prophet mighty in deed and word before God and all the people, and how our chief priests and leaders handed him over to be condemned to death and crucified him. (Luke 24.19–20)

Then something interesting happens. Jesus goes over the story they know so well, the whole story, the story of faith. He goes over that story from the beginning. He tells them what they know, he explores an experience that is already familiar. But this time their hearts burn within them:

> beginning with Moses and all the prophets, he interpreted to them the things about himself in all the scriptures. (Luke 24.27)

It is the same story, but differently understood. Even then, the disciples do not *see* Jesus. That comes later, in a eucharistic moment, at a table. That recognition is crucial, it is very significant, but it is not the end of the story. The thing that should give us pause is what happens next. The disciples leave Emmaus and go back to Jerusalem. What has changed is the direction of travel. Easter is not another event. Easter is an explanation, and Easter is a direction of travel.

The disciples walking to Emmaus were quite right. Their disappointment was real. History is a record littered with failures and with violence. History does not point us anywhere. Our history, and the cross that looms over it, says something profoundly important to us. Disappointment, suffering and tragedy are not an aberration, or the consequence of sin or bad luck. They are all woven deep into our experience. We do suffer. We are not deceived. When God enters history, God, in the person of Christ, suffers. That does not stop being true at Easter. There is still pain, there is still suffering. Easter is not another event, the next bit of the historical sequence. Easter is God's judgement on history. It is another way of seeing; a different direction of travel.

Notes

1 Available online at https://www.church of england.org/prayer-and-worship/worship-texts-and-resources/common-worship/churchs-year/holy-week-and-easter/easter-liturgy.
2 C. Wordsworth, 'Alleluia! Alleluia!'
3 C. Wesley, 'Love's redeeming work is done'.

Ascension
A risen and ascended life

Looking up

On a cold January day in 1649, King Charles I walked across the floor of the Banqueting House in Whitehall. He was on his way to the scaffold which had been built outside. Having walked to Whitehall across St James's Park, he had then been forced to wait for three long hours. No one had executed a king before and there were all sorts of anxieties about who was, and was not, prepared to put their name to such a startling act. This was an extraordinary moment for an entire nation; but for Charles, of course, it was a very personal crisis. Now, with the hope of heaven very much on his mind he made a short but extraordinary journey. We cannot know if Charles dragged his eyes away from the window and the scaffold that lay beyond it, and instead looked up. It would have been odd if he had not at least glanced at a very famous ceiling and an image of his own father. Above him, and installed relatively recently, there was a painting of the glory of royal majesty, Rubens' *Apotheosis of James I*. James, seated in heaven, now looked down on this majesty brought low.

That picture of James I was a measure of the ambition of the monarchy. Charles would have had to crane his neck to see it. Aspiration always looks up; it is the reason we use the phrase 'things are looking up'. We have 'high hopes'. It is a fundamental assumption for us that ambition will get us to the top. Any artist thinking about heavenly glory will also assume that it happens over our heads. Go to Rome, stand under the arch of Titus and look up. There is an image of Titus on the back of an eagle. It was put there in the summit of the arch 1,500 years before Rubens began the painting for the Banqueting House. It is another apotheosis; Titus is about to become one of the gods. To do that, he will fly upwards.

There is a presiding idea that heaven is above us and that hope looks upwards. The idea that our belief will direct us upwards is familiar; it is bred in the bone. Ascension Day, then, seems to tell us what we knew all along. To complete his ministry Christ has to go *up*. Hymns make the point, as in Charles Wesley's 'Hail the day':

Hail the day that sees him rise
Glorious to his native skies

There is a particularly interesting idea there that Jesus came from the sky and is going back there. Thomas Kelly's Ascension hymn, 'The head that once was crowned with thorns', avoids that pitfall, but has us singing,

The highest place that heaven affords
Is his, is his by right

Ascension Day routinely has us thinking about Jesus going up. If you are still in any doubt about this, a trip to Walsingham might help. There, in the Chapel of the Ascension (in the Anglican shrine) you can savour the sight of Christ's feet sticking out of the ceiling. Ascension is the day when we look up, because Jesus has gone up to heaven.

Well, not quite. You do not need to have a further degree in astrophysics to know that there is a difficulty in claiming that heaven is 'up there'. There is also a more serious problem here. The consequence of all this looking up is that we make an assumption about the fact that we are down here and heaven (and the ascended Christ) is up there. Thomas Kelly's hymn also contains the lines:

The joy of all who dwell above,
The joy of all below . . .

They suffer with their Lord below,
They reign with him above.

There are two distinct, different realities here and one of them
is above the other. We set God at a distance. That is an understandable mistake, but it really is a mistake. Make the first mistake and a lot more mistakes follow quickly.

Once we put God *above*, we then naturally think that God
looks down and surveys the scene. Much as you or I might
look down on a chessboard before we decide to move one of
the pieces, God, it seems, surveys the world. It is at this point
that the image gets us into real trouble because God now turns
into an eternal chief executive, a decision-maker in a penthouse
office with pearly gates at the lift door. We have been making
that assumption for a long time. The world in which the New
Testament was written was a world that believed that there were
many gods who had just this kind of power. There were gods of
harvest and gods of battle, gods of good luck, gods of love, and
gods of storm and sea. If good things happened, if you found
a key you had lost, or made a fortune, it was because the gods
decreed it. If bad things happened, if you got toothache, or your
house was blown away by a typhoon, it was because the gods
willed it. There was no rhyme or reason to these events; the gods
were fickle, even faithless. All that was known was that they
looked down on us and made decisions about us. They lived
apart. We may not believe in those gods now, but the old idea
surfaces from time to time and in some surprising places. I may
have been the only person at the stage performance of *Mamma
Mia* who thought the theology of the script was interesting, but
there it was again. The song 'The Winner Takes It All' is about
love and fate. It includes the line:

The gods may throw the dice.

It is not just a romantic notion that we are subject to heavenly powers. Tom Wright has pointed out that we hear this language, in different dress, when we listen to the news.

> Who runs our world? The politicians? Forget it. They profess themselves helpless; they are victims of 'forces' beyond their control . . . It's all a matter of economic forces.[1]

The language we use about 'the market', assuring ourselves that 'the market will decide' and wondering what 'market forces' might do, is language that our ancestors would recognize. Christians are not immune from thinking that God is somewhere 'up there' and makes decisions about us. We are used to setting God at a distance, and having done that we assume that Ascension Day is the moment when Jesus leaves to be with a God who remains, resolutely, 'up there'.

The problem is that we have confused two ideas. We need to make a distinction. Christians know that God is not 'like' us. It is very important that we do know this. There is a thrilling moment in the Book of Job when God speaks out of a whirlwind to silence the bickering explanations being offered as descriptions of what God is like:

> I will question you, and you shall declare to me. Where were you when I laid the foundation of the earth? Tell me, if you have understanding. Who determined its measurements – surely you know! . . . Or who shut in the sea with doors when it burst out from the womb? – when I made the clouds its garment, and thick darkness its swaddling band, and prescribed bounds for it, and set bars and doors, and said, 'Thus far shall you come, and no farther, and here shall your proud waves be stopped'? Have you commanded the morning since your days began, and caused the dawn to know its place, so that it might take hold of the skirts of the earth, and the wicked be shaken out of it? (Job 38.3–13)

It is an article of faith in the Hebrew scriptures that God is not like anything else and is certainly not like us.

> To whom then will you compare me, or who is my equal? says the Holy One. Lift up your eyes on high and see: Who created these? He who brings out their host and numbers them, calling them all by name; because he is great in strength, mighty in power, not one is missing. Why do you say, O Jacob, and speak, O Israel, 'My way is hidden from the LORD, and my right is disregarded by my God'? Have you not known? Have you not heard? The LORD is the everlasting God, the Creator of the ends of the earth. He does not faint or grow weary; his understanding is unsearchable. He gives power to the faint, and strengthens the powerless. Even youths will faint and be weary, and the young will fall exhausted. (Isaiah 40.25–30)

Set apart

When we call God 'holy' this is what we mean. Holiness is a kind of separation; holy things are set apart. We are clear that God is not like us. God is apart from us. In Jesus, God draws close. We encounter God in a form we can understand (he is made like us), but we still need to be clear that we have not *apprehended* God. We have seen the Son; we have not known the Father.

> No one has ever seen God. It is God the only Son, who is close to the Father's heart, who has made him known. (John 1.18)

God is *apart* from us, though being apart is not the same as being remote or 'above'. This is the confusion we slip into. Knowing that God is not like us, we make the separation between us physical. We would do better to think of a God who is different in *kind*, not in a different *space*.

Read the first chapter of the Epistle of James and you will find the author thinking hard about the way human beings deceive themselves. James has a lot to say about us being unstable, tempted, lured, deceived. It is only a swift aside, but he notes that God is not like that. God is

> the Father of lights, with whom there is no variation or shadow due to change. (James 1.17)

We are different from God. We struggle with circumstance all the time, we are prone to moods, we react to change. We can be by turns loving, angry, anxious, passionate or doubtful. God is not like that. God is, in a sense, much simpler than we are. God is constant: constantly loving, constantly compassionate. It is in this sense that God is not like us and *apart* from us.

Muddled in our assumptions about where God is to be found, what it means for God to be apart, we get Ascension Day badly wrong.

We need to note the instruction given at the beginning of the Acts of the Apostles:

> [Jesus] was lifted up, and a cloud took him out of their sight. While he was going and they were gazing up towards heaven, suddenly two men in white robes stood by them. They said, 'Men of Galilee, why do you stand looking up towards heaven?' (Acts 1.9–11)

The point made in Acts is that the Disciples must not get stranded in a faith that looks up. They are to go back to Jerusalem; they are told that Christ will come to them again. St Luke makes the same point in the Gospel (Luke wrote his Gospel and the Acts of the Apostles). At the Ascension, the Disciples return to Jerusalem and praise God. The story does not end with Jesus *going away*. The story continues precisely where it was.

What Luke wants us to know, and he really wants us to know this, is that there has only ever been one story: a continuous story of God's abiding relationship with us. So, on the Emmaus road, or with the Ethiopian eunuch on the way to Gaza, or in the penultimate scene from the Gospel, at the lakeside before the Ascension, the explanation always takes in the whole story:

> These are my words that I spoke to you while I was still with you – that everything written about me in the law of Moses, the prophets, and the psalms must be fulfilled. (Luke 24.44)

The story that began with Moses and the prophets is not overturned, or replaced, nor is it cancelled out. Instead the story is *fulfilled*. In fact, we begin before Moses. Luke gives us a genealogy of Jesus that takes the story back to 'Adam, son of God' (Luke 3.38). The Ascension is absolutely not a break in this crucial continuity, as though God lived among us and then went away. What happens at the Ascension is that Jesus joins our life to God, for ever. It is not unreasonable to say that this is the moment that Jesus *lifts* our life into God. The crucial thing, however, is to recognize that there can never be an *up there* and *down here* again. Here is Tom Wright again:

> Heaven is the extra dimension, the God-dimension, of all our present reality; and the God who lives there is present to us, present with us, sharing our joys and our sorrows, longing as we are longing for the day when his whole creation, heaven and earth together, will perfectly reflect his love, his wisdom, his justice, and his peace.
>
> The ascension of Jesus, then, is his going, not way beyond the stars, but into this space, this dimension. Notice what this does to our notion of heaven. The Jesus who has gone there is the human Jesus. People sometimes talk as if Jesus started off just being divine, then stopped being divine and became human, then stopped being human and went back to being divine again. That is precisely what the ascension rules out.[2]

Ascension Day tells us that human life is now inseparable from the life of God. As Rowan Williams puts it:

the humanity that we all know to be stained, wounded, imprisoned in various ways; this humanity – yours and mine – is still capable of being embraced by God, shot through with God's glory, received and welcomed in the burning heart of reality itself.[3]

We started with Rubens in the Banqueting House; let me offer you another picture. In the Bavarian National Museum in Munich there is a little ivory carving made round about the year 400 (it is usually called the *Munich Ivory of the Ascension* if you want to look it up). It combines two stories we know very well. At the bottom left stands the empty tomb (looking perhaps a little more elaborate than we imagined). There are sleeping soldiers, and we can see the two women who have come to the tomb, and the angel who says to them:

Why do you look for the living among the dead? He is not here, but has risen. (Luke 24.5)

In the top right-hand corner is the second scene, and it is the Ascension. It is the Ascension understood a little differently. Christ strides up a hillside, his cloak billowing behind him. His right hand is extended and he grasps the hand of God as it emerges from a cloud. He does not take off like a rocket and disappear into the cloud (or the ceiling). He puts his hand into the hand of God; they are joined. This ivory understands the continuity that matters so much. The risen life of Jesus, the story we have been told about him eating and being seen and touched after the resurrection; that story goes on. Jesus takes that life into the life of God. In those two clasped hands heaven meets earth. The human life of Jesus is joined to the life of the Father, and taken not just into heaven but into the heart of God.

At Ascension your life and mine are lifted into the deeper, loving, merciful reality of God. Human life and divine life are united. That is why creeds tell us that Jesus is 'seated at the right hand of the Father'. The emphasis is not on the fact that he went up, the emphasis falls on the fact that his life is the life of God. Like the clasped hands of the ivory they are held there. Rowan Williams imagines Jesus, in his humanity, coming to the Father and saying:

> This is the humanity I have brought home. It's not a pretty sight; it's not edifying and impressive and heroic, it's just real: real and needy and confused, and here it is (this complicated humanity) brought home to heaven, dropped into the burning heart of God – for healing and for transformation.[4]

Notes

1 N. T. Wright, *Following Jesus* (London: SPCK, 1994), p. 12.

2 Wright, *Following Jesus*, p. 86.

3 R. Williams, 'A Sermon by the Archbishop of Canterbury at the Ascension Day Sung Eucharist, May 2009', http://aoc2013.brix.fatbeehive.com/articles.php/883/a-sermon-by-the-archbishop-of-canterbury-at-the-ascension-day-sung-eucharist (accessed 4 March 2019).

4 Williams, 'A Sermon by the Archbishop'.

I2

Pentecost

The words and wisdom to hold it together

Years ago, when I was Dean of a Cambridge college, I tried a number of incentives to tempt people into chapel. A famous name coming to preach at evensong, perhaps, or a glass of witheringly dry sherry afterwards. In the morning, I could offer breakfast after chapel. If it were a feast day, this would be breakfast washed down with Buck's Fizz. This was the inducement that worked best. We had some rather jolly feast days, and among them Pentecost was a favourite. If Easter was late, Pentecost arrived as exams were finishing, and then the Buck's Fizz would keep flowing until I called 'time'. So it was that one of the more godly members of my congregation came to chapel, joined enthusiastically in the festal breakfast, and then went on to another church service in town. There, he heard the familiar reading from Acts: the Apostles speaking in tongues and the allegation that they must have been drinking new wine.

> But Peter, standing with the eleven, raised his voice and addressed them: 'Men of Judea . . . Indeed, these are not drunk, as you suppose, for it is only nine o'clock in the morning.' (Acts 2.14–15)

My chapel-goer looked at his watch. It was a little after ten o'clock.

We count the weeks from Easter to reach Pentecost. In truth, it has its roots in Jewish observance. The word 'Pentecost' means 'fiftieth'. This is the fiftieth day after Passover, and for

the Jews it was the day of the 'feast of weeks' (more usually
called Shavuot). It is the day on which faithful Jews celebrate
the giving of the Law on Sinai. That was why Jerusalem was
crowded on this particular day and why so many different languages were being spoken, 'every nation under heaven'.

Because the Spirit conferred the gift of speech on the Apostles
in Jerusalem, you might suppose that we have plenty to say
about the Spirit. In truth, the Spirit is mysterious. Like a cat
burglar, the Spirit is not seen, but you know where he has been.
Jesus describes the Spirit in deliberately mysterious terms:

> This is the Spirit of truth, whom the world cannot receive,
> because it neither sees him nor knows him. (John 14.17)

We should notice that the Spirit gives the Apostles the ability to speak 'about God's deeds of power' (Acts 2.11). The
Spirit does not speak of itself. I have friends who have not quite
learnt that lesson; I have sat with them as they have spoken
of themselves at length. I do it myself, and far too often. The
Spirit, though, is self-effacing:

> When the Spirit of truth comes, he will guide you into all the
> truth; for he will not speak on his own, but will speak what-
> ever he hears. (John 16.13)

If you have ever found the Holy Spirit elusive, or slightly tricky,
you can forgive yourself. The Spirit *is* elusive. Our conversation about the Spirit should be a little more hesitant than it
sometimes is.

To think about the Spirit we need to think about where the
Spirit has been. Years ago, in that college where we celebrated
with Buck's Fizz, I met a first-year student called Duncan. We
had conversations that still stay with me. We did not talk about
faith or exchange biblical quotations. He did not have much
faith, and during a serious illness he had had a bad experience
of priests. Duncan was reading English; we used to talk about
poems a fair bit. He knew many poems I did not know, some of

them tough to understand. One of them, however, 'Snow', by Louis MacNeice. I came to love very quickly. Before going any further, I should explain that MacNeice was not the sort of poet who wafted through banks of daffodils being wistful. He had a disastrous love life and a much more consistent affection for alcohol. His life was a racket. That was awkward. MacNeice's father was pious, a Northern Ireland Anglican who became a bishop. One grey winter's day in his father's rather dour house, the young MacNeice looked out of the window. He looked past a dramatic bunch of pink roses on the windowsill to a snow-storm beyond. It was a chaotic image, tumbling snow outside, cut flowers within; an intrusion on sullen routine. MacNeice wrote of the world being 'crazier',

and more of it than we think.[1]

The poem, and a lot more besides, was one element in Duncan's parting gift to me. He did not live long after that conversation. He had good reason to be a commentator on the craziness of life.

Now, I spend my working life as a dean. I have oversight of a cathedral. Cathedrals are complicated places. At any given moment, on a Tuesday morning, say, you might have 20 children practising Bairstow in D somewhere over there, while here you might have a verger polishing his aspergillum (you can look that up later). Over there is a slightly odd young man who has perhaps taken something that was not good for him and wants to persuade you that he is, indeed, the Son of God. Down there are two earnest tourists discussing the dif-ference between an arch and an ambo. Up there the organist is practising a phrase from Messiaen for the fourteenth time, and here, in front of you, is someone in floods of tears because her mother is in an operating theatre at the Royal Infirmary. The world really does feel crazy, 'and more of it than we think'. You tidy all this up at your peril, because much of it is the work of the Spirit. When the boat club passed through the col-lege I worked in on the night of their dinner, they left behind

one thing: disorder. Where the Spirit has been, what you get is
abundance and variety. God is generous and loves abundance:

and more of it than we think.

Read Genesis and you will find that it is the Spirit that gave
us abundance. Genesis starts with a formless deep, the surge
of the sea, and the Spirit brings out of the deep this which is
different from that, and then something else. It is the sheer
abundance of creation that we are supposed to notice and
celebrate. This is the Spirit that *does* that. It is the Spirit that
has the Apostles speaking in all those different tongues at
Pentecost.

Why does that matter? Well, it matters because in our determination to be 'on message' we lose our enthusiasm for variety.
Now and again, as we name our priorities and pursue the strategy, it sounds as though we all aspire to be the same. Schools
and dioceses, like businesses, have straplines – 'together aiming
high' or, 'we believe we will achieve'. I used to have a motto on
my school blazer but it was in Latin and I never knew what it
meant. I am pretty sure no one ever thought to tell me. Books
tell me that there are five habits of successful people, or three
steps to getting my own way. Meanwhile, the Spirit, active in
creation, moves over the face of the waters and separates this
from that; God's abundance breaks out all around us. Turning
to another poet, Gerard Manley Hopkins, we are supposed to
like the fact that it is not all the same:

All things counter, original, spare, strange;
Whatever is fickle, freckled (who knows how?)[2]

The great challenge is that we should be different and enjoy
it: different and interested, different and working away at a
language to hold and celebrate all that difference. The day of
Pentecost, the day of the Spirit, is the day we celebrate the fact
that God gives us variety, *and* gives us the gifts of imagination and language to make us into a community. In the Spirit

we can forgive, explain, argue and be reconciled, we can cooperate, sympathize and love.

That first Pentecost, the gift of speech broke out in a city crowded with different nations. They were there to celebrate the giving of the Law. They were there, in fact, to acknowledge that God offers us order as well as abundance. The Spirit is lively and abundant. When we say that someone is 'spirited' or 'animated' we are using the language of the Spirit to acknowledge that they are energetic. That is the life that Jesus breathes into his disciples. Yet, the same Spirit holds all this abundance and energy in unity. The Spirit is never chaos. The Spirit, in creation, brought order out of chaos, distinguishing one thing from another. The Spirit that provides words and wisdom is what interprets, and reconciles. The Spirit is constantly at work communicating truth and understanding.

Pentecost is the day of variety and day of understanding. It summons us to see where the Spirit has been.

Notes

1 L. MacNeice, 'Snow' in *Collected Poems* (London: Faber, 1966), p. 30.

2 G. M. Hopkins, 'Pied Beauty' in *Gerard Manley Hopkins* (London: Folio Society, 1974), p. 68.

13

Trinity

Every day in the Trinity

In Rome, about 100 metres south of the crowds thronging the
Piazza Navona, stands the church of Sant' Andrea della Valle
(you will have to dawdle if you are going to finish your ice
cream before you go inside). When you do enter, you will find
the walls and the roof ablaze with gold leaf. Where there is no
gold leaf, there is painting. There are cherubs and martyrs and
confessors, all rushing towards heaven. In the middle of this
riot, there is a dome. Look up and you will see the Virgin Mary
being assumed into heaven. It is breathtaking. You are looking straight into heaven, and of course it puts a strain on the
neck. Looking at heaven is always problematic. The painter
of this dome, Giovanni Lanfranco, thought that this was his
masterpiece. Other people thought so too – all those clever
perspectives and the bravura composition. Then the theologians came, with narrowing eyes alert to error. Lanfranco
had filled heaven with saints, all them watching Mary arrive
in glory. And the theologians pointed out that he had got it
wrong. Some of those saints should not be there – they could
not possibly have already been there waiting for Mary; she
died before they did.

Lanfranco got into trouble because he tried to show us one
specific moment in heaven. He tried to show us a bit of history,
the day Mary died and arrived in glory. The problem is that
there is no history in heaven; heaven is eternal. The saints are
there for ever. There are no Tuesdays in heaven, no yesterday,

no 'coming soon', no 'later on'. That is very hard to paint; it is very difficult for us to even *think* about God's throne. Our words, our concepts, are not up to the job. Each Trinity Sunday this is the problem we must negotiate, as we set out to describe the nature of God.

Trinity Sunday is not one of the ancient feasts of the Church. In the eleventh century, Pope Alexander II argued that the idea of a Sunday dedicated to the Trinity was a nonsense. We say 'Glory to the Father and to the Son and to the Holy Spirit' every day, he said; the Trinity is proclaimed in every liturgy. He was making an important point, but a tide of devotion was running against him. By 1334, a successor, John XXII, ordered that the Feast of the Trinity should be kept on the Sunday after Pentecost.

Pope Alexander understood that all day, every day, we live *within* the Trinity. On other feast days we tell a story. At Pentecost, we can read about the Apostles speaking in tongues. On their saint's day, we could tell the story of Ambrose, or Augustine; we could put them in context, explain their significance. On Trinity Sunday, however, we cannot do that. This is a day when context eludes us. When we want to get to grips with something complicated, we talk about *getting perspective*, *finding an angle*. When it is getting near lunchtime and you are 40 minutes into a tricky debate about margins, risks and priorities, someone is bound to suggest we 'step back'. You cannot do that with the Trinity. The Trinity is simply not a story we can tell. The Trinity is the story *about* us. The Trinity is our beginning and our end, our meaning and our existence. We can no more get an angle on the Trinity than a halibut can get an angle on the ocean.

We have no perspective, no angle, on God. We could never *frame* an argument about what God is like, as though God might be contained. Nor can we *compare* God to anything else. That is a point that Isaiah made long ago:

To whom then will you liken God, or what likeness compare with him? (Isaiah 40.18)

We say that God is *mighty* or *wise*, but if we begin to think that this makes God a bit like the Incredible Hulk or Maya Angelou, then we are headed into a theological cul-de-sac. So, we need to recognize that despite all the books we have written and all the sermons that have been preached, we do not know God. Christians (and indeed Muslims and Jews) are the people who know that they do not know God. Description and explanation will always fail.

We do not know God. There are, however, some things that we can say about God. The first of them, and the place you must start on Trinity Sunday, is that God is *one*. As well as insisting that God is not like anything else, Isaiah declared that there could be nothing alongside God, nothing before God, nothing to inform God:

> Have you not known? Have you not heard? Has it not been told you from the beginning? Have you not understood from the foundations of the earth? (Isaiah 40.21)

There are not lots of explanations, there is *one*. Christians do not believe in the gods. We do not believe in fate, or good luck; we do not believe in Mother Earth, or crystals, or The Market. We do not believe in a God who has only partial oversight, or particular concerns, as though God might like the English and dislike the French. There are no exceptions, no oversights, no accidents under God, as though God is a God of sunrise and sunset but not of cancer or crucifixion. We believe in *one* God.

Our God is not one of the gods, not one explanation among others, not a thing to set against another thing. Everything that has happened and will happen, all existence, every idea I have, all your hopes and dreams – they all exist simply and only because of the God who creates and tells us *you must have no other gods but me*. That is important. In all the confusion of processes we cannot master, and amid narratives that spool out of control, we live in fear and in confusion. Because we can see no solution and no story, we introduce boundaries that make us feel safer and more powerful. We talk about 'fake news' and decide who we will and will not trust. We see the world as 'them' and 'us'. We make politics more local, we locate ourselves within communities of shared conviction and reinforce association with a hashtag. Yet, if we truly believe in one God, we must believe in the absolute integrity of all that is. Despite all the evidence to the contrary, there must still be a common narrative. It must still be the case that we are more united than divided: everything that is with a single point of origin and a single destination.

It is for these reasons that we have slipped into the habit of calling God 'Father'. The language is flawed; it is limited. God might be *like* a Father, but of course God is nothing like the way I am a father, affectionate and grumpy by turns, and just possibly prone to cheating at games of Cluedo. We use this language because it is the best we have. God is like a Father because (for some of us at least) the image of a father who precedes and protects conveys some ideas about how the story holds together.

That is the first thing we say about God. On Trinity Sunday, we say God is one. We also say (and say it very quickly) that God is three. We do that because the God we can never know makes known the existence we could not describe. God is a God who reveals. From what God reveals there are things we *can* know. We say that God creates. All that exists, exists because God pours himself out in creation. We go on to say that the God who creates is also a God who communicates. You could, I suppose, have a God who creates and then retires into hiding. Our God pours himself out. God *speaks*. 'In the beginning was the word,' says St John. God does not turn inward, but proceeds out and issues a word. The word that God speaks is Jesus. Which changes everything. The love that is at the heart of all things, the mysterious love of a Creator that pours itself out in the joyful business of creating, is also the love we encounter in a human being, Jesus. The God we cannot know, the love we cannot describe, we meet in Jesus and we recognize it. Notice that Jesus is not created; he is not a *creature*. He has the same life of the Father and in him that life, the life of God himself, is perfectly united to the lively and messy business of being human. And then we say, that mysterious life and love of the Father, which is lived in front of us by the Son, is also lived within us. We do not just see it, we participate. We are drawn into that life and love. That is the third thing we know. We know that the life of God breathes in us, that we are taken up into the life of God. That is the work of the Spirit.

God is one and God is three. We must say, and go on saying, that both those statements are true. Err one way and you have three gods; err the other and you have one God simply operating in three different ways. God is one, but God is three persons, Father, Son and Spirit. There is a real distinction and a real relationship between the three. There is, indeed, a relationship of love at the heart of all that is.

We may not know God. We do not know God. But we know what we need to know. We know that the God who is always and utterly one is also three. We have to say that the one God is a Trinity. The one God is Father, Son and Spirit. The one God in whom and for whom all things exist is visible in Christ, and is at work within us living his life in us. We have to say that God is one and that God is three. Anything less is less than the truth. Anything else fails to assert the fundamental truth that relationship and unity lie at the heart of all that is.

And Pope Alexander was right – every day is a day lived in the glory of the Trinity.

14

Ordinary Time

Neither feast day nor fast

> We have done with dogma and divinity.
> Easter and Whitsun past
> The long, long Sundays after Trinity
> Are with us at last;
> The passionless Sundays after Trinity
> Neither feast-day nor fast.[1]

The poet John Meade Falkner thought that it was just the 'long, long Sundays after Trinity', but it turns out to be a bit more complicated than that. Ordinary Time, after the great sequence of feast and fast, is a different routine. The complications of it might excite liturgists, writing in their diaries with coloured pens, and very small letters, but it is hardly an idea that makes other hearts beat faster. That poem does not promise much.

> But these are five and twenty,
> The longest Sundays of all;
> The placid Sundays after Trinity,
> Wheat-harvest, fruit-harvest, Fall.

Which rather begs the question of what we expect of the Christian year and how 'ordinary' we expect our time to be. There are, in fact, two periods of Ordinary Time in each year. One of them begins after Epiphany and ends before Lent. As I explained earlier, the Church of England has recently got enthusiastic about Epiphany, so if you are Roman Catholic this period starts on the day after the Baptism of Christ, but if you are an Anglican you must wait until the day after the Presentation of Christ in the Temple. The second period of Ordinary Time falls in those long weeks after Trinity Sunday. With Ordinary Time, there is a new routine. If vestments are worn they will now be green (in Epiphany and on Trinity Sunday you wear white). If your church follows the cycle of readings from the lectionary, you should notice that after all the excitement of special readings for special days, you are now staying with particular books of the Bible, reading them in sequence.

Ordinary does not get a good press. No one, at the moment, would aspire to be merely *ordinary*. There are too many books, too many posters, urging us to step up and do better. In life, in relationship, in faith, only extra-ordinary is good enough. There is an urgent voice that will not let us settle for the commonplace and normal. The best of these voices say something we should hear. They remind us that we should look for glimpses of glory all around. The extraordinary really is never far away. That is why the poet Mary Oliver wanted to be a bride 'married to amazement'[2] and why Michael Mayne could write a book called *This Sunrise of Wonder*. God's creation bears the imprint of God's glory, what Gerard Manley Hopkins thought of as 'God's grandeur'. For that reason, of course, we should never consider anyone ordinary. The psalmist was quite right to say, 'I praise you, for I am fearfully and wonderfully made' (Psalm 139.14).

Much less welcome, however, is a hyperinflation of the spirit. There is a thoroughly modern heresy in the idea that Christian spirituality requires us to live at a constant breathless pitch. We are encouraged to believe that every experience might be announced by trumpets and bathed in a golden glow. It is as though, with a little more effort, we could step into Narnia at will. If only we tried, we could all live in a better, deeper reality and *shine*. To understand why this is mistaken (and actually dangerous) we need to understand creation. We also need to learn to live in ordinary time.

On 30 January 1896, the French entomologist Jean Henri Fabre was studying pine processionary moth caterpillars in his garden. When these creatures set out to feed, they do it in single file, nose to tail (allow me that licence, even I know that caterpillars have neither). Fabre watched a large group crawl up the side of a large flower pot. At the top, they set off round the rim, and then Fabre pushed away the rest of the column. He was left with a circular procession marching round and round. Despite having no food or water, they pressed on and on. Each night as the temperature fell they slowed to a halt and each morning, with sunrise, they would resume the endless circle. Day after day it continued until, famished, they began to tumble from the rim.

Writing about Fabre's experiment years later, Annie Dillard suggested:

> It is the fixed that horrifies us, the fixed that assails us with the tremendous force of its mindlessness.[3]

She was telling us how terrible systems and processes can be, how destructive it would be to be caught in something *fixed*. She was also making a point about the kind of agent who intervenes from outside, controls and constrains. She compared Fabre's experiment to the story of Elijah mocking the prophets of Baal – the ones who danced round a woodpile, slashing at their own skin, calling down fire from heaven, but the wood stayed wood and the fire never came.

> What street-corner vendor wound the key on the backs of tin soldiers and abandoned them to the sidewalk, and crashings over the curb?[4]

This is the reason we turn against the *ordinary*. We rebel against routine and constraint. Worse still, we worry, like Annie Dillard, about the someone, or the something, that must be behind the crushing constraint. This is the image we cannot get out of our heads when we think of creation. We keep assuming that, interesting as the world around us is, just over the rain-bow there is a boss who is in charge of it all. The language we use, of *creation* and a *creator*, encourages us to think that there is a thing (creation) and a God who sits above it somehow, or (worse) potters in and out, fixing some things, ignoring others. We also assume that there is another, better reality just out of sight and that with a bit more effort we can get there. We find the ordinary wanting and start reaching for the stars. We are confused. Let us be clear, God is not the boss. God does not sit, just out of sight, making a decision on Tuesday and having a new idea on Friday. We really must rid ourselves of the desire to turn God into the CEO of creation-enterprises.com.

To break ourselves of this habit we need to take a deep breath and plunge into a deeper understanding of what theology has always said about creation. When you, or I, make something, we fashion one thing into something else. We make a cake out of ingredients and thus turn one thing into another. Creation is not like that. God does not change raw materials into something else. Theologians at their (rather intense) sherry parties always say that God creates *ex nihilo*. That is, God creates *out of nothing*. It is a point that Thomas Aquinas makes. It is not just that creation is something that uniquely belongs to God, or that creating is a thing God alone does. The idea here is that everything has its origin in God and depends on God for ever. There is no 'stuff' that God found lying about and then turned into something else. God, always and for ever, relates to creation not as the 'boss', nor as an agent that might change it, but as its origin and its destination. It also follows that you would never arrive at God if you added all creation up. God is not *part* of creation, nor the sum of its parts. So, it is not helpful to think of *before* and *after*, as though we might identify a moment of creation and imagine a moment after. Nor is it helpful to separate God from what is created. Creation springs from God eternally and creation surges into God in equal time. What this means is that anything we might wish to consider *ordinary* is, in truth, utterly inseparable from God. If we go looking for something else, something more, we are missing the point. The understandable longing to be *extraordinary* actually rests on a refusal to accept things as they are and live in creation as it is given.

The familiar story from Genesis is so contested that we argue simply over whether it is true or false. That is a shame. If we took time to read it differently and more generously we might notice some surprising insights. So, for example, in Genesis, the pinnacle of creation turns out to be the Sabbath when God rests. There is no urgency to go one better, to try harder; the truly faithful thing to do is to see the good in what already is.

> God saw everything that he had made, and indeed, it was very good. (Genesis 1.31)

Ordinary Time is anything but dull. It asks of us to commit fully to life here and now. It asks us to commit to living in a creation springing from God and returning to God. This creation is inseparable from God, it is full of God's power and God's presence. Acknowledging that power and that presence, *really* acknowledging the life and energy that rushes through creation, would be overwhelming. The truth is that the ordinary is overwhelming. It is something George Eliot understood and explained in *Middlemarch*:

> If we had a keen vision and feeling of all ordinary human life, it would be like hearing the grass grow and the squirrel's heart beat, and we should die of that roar which lies on the other side of silence. As it is, the quickest of us walk about well wadded with stupidity.[5]

Living in ordinary time, we resist the terrible temptation to think we would do better somewhere else. If only I could be free of these constraints, that challenge, these people, I could finally become the person I ought to be. It is a temptation the desert fathers knew well. The feeling is called *acedia*, and it always longs to be somewhere else.

Of course, that longing is not entirely misplaced. God's creation strives for fulfilment. It is not what it will be. God's future will bring reconciliation, redemption and restoration. We long for that and all creation. As St Paul points out, creation itself 'waits with eager longing for the revealing of the children of God' (Romans 8.19). A whole season of the year, Advent, is given over to exploring the idea that we feel a dislocation between what is and what will be. We must be clear, though, that what we long for is the future, the completion and fulfilment of what is. We are not pursuing a different reality as though we belong somewhere else.

Notes

1 J. M. Falkner, from 'After Trinity', partially quoted in P. H. Pfatteicher, *Journey into the Heart of God: Living the Liturgical Year* (Oxford: Oxford University Press, 2013), p. 302. The full poem can be found online at www.poemhunter.com/poem/after-trinity/.

2 M. Oliver, 'When Death Comes' in *New and Selected Poems*, Vol. 1 (Boston, MA: Beacon Press, 1992).

3 A. Dillard, *Pilgrim at Tinker Creek* (New York: Harper Perennial, 1974), pp. 68–9.

4 Dillard, *Pilgrim at Tinker Creek*, p. 68.

5 G. Eliot, *Middlemarch* (London: Penguin, 1965), p. 226.

15

All Saints

The holiness of others, the otherness of holiness

I took a funeral, years ago, at Golders Green crematorium. Here the coffin leaves the chapel by moving slowly, from the central catafalque, to a door in the wall off to one side. It is carried on a kind of conveyer belt and every eye is usually fixed upon it. At this particular service we had gathered to pray for a Lancastrian, a man of wide reading and old loyalties. He had asked that the funeral end with Gracie Fields singing 'Sally, Sally, pride of our alley'. There was a mistake made somewhere. We sat, not daring to catch each other's eye, as the coffin moved slowly past us to the sound of Our Gracie belting out, 'Wish me luck, as you wave me goodbye'.

We summon up these songs that we play at funerals, all those recordings of 'My Way', or 'Wind Beneath My Wings', because the shared memory restores the dead, brings them back into our company. I have spent years, preaching beside a coffin, explaining that the dead have not 'done with us', their relationship with us goes on. Poems and readings made familiar at funerals urge us to hang on to the affection that death has fractured. So, Henry Scott Holland gets wheeled out again: 'There is absolute and unbroken continuity . . . I am but waiting for you, for an interval, somewhere very near, just round the corner.'[1] Others, though, have not been so confident, are quicker to suggest that the dead are lost to us, isolated. It is this different, bleaker voice we hear in John Donne's 'Death's Duel'. He describes the man that strove to take control, the one that 'thought himself his own for ever'. Even this man will come to nothing:

> mingled with the dust of every highway and of every dung-hill, and swallowed in every puddle and pond. This is the most inglorious and contemptible vilification, the most deadly and peremptory nullification of man . . .[2]

It is this challenge that the saints equip us to meet.

We meet the saints as statues or as pictures: St Francis in ecstasy, St Katharine and her wheel. Or we meet them as stories: Kevin and the blackbird or Christina the Astonishing floating up to the rafters. Some of the images, some of the stories, get a grip on us. We go to modern saints like Oscar Romero, Janani Luwum, and we learn about faith or hope or courage. There is a lesson to take away, something we can use, make our own. Other saints, like Christina the Astonishing for instance, leave us more perplexed (look her up). We are not sure what it is we should learn. We cannot appropriate what we find.

Oddly, it is from the very 'otherness' of Christina the Astonishing that we are more likely to learn what we need to know. The point about the saints is that they offer us a glimpse of what we so struggle to see. The saints show us what holiness looks like. We go to the saints hoping to have something to carry away, something to make our own. The saints became saints, however, precisely because they could *not* be accommodated, or tamed. The saints will never belong to us; they always belong to themselves and to God. They are holy. They remind us that holy things are separate and set apart. As Aquinas tells us, holy things also have something firm about them. They will not be altered, or deflected.

In each generation, in different places and in very different ways, the saints, women and men made like us, show us what holiness looks like. They show us that holiness takes different forms. The most notable thing about the saints is that they are so different from one another (except in the sense that they are all holy and were, in different ways, *firm*). They make an extraordinary community. The Feast of All Saints, properly understood, beggars belief. How could you possibly begin to describe all that crazy variety, what possible story could you tell?

Yet, of one thing we are sure, and that is that the saints make a community. We do think of them as a company. We think that in their holiness and their firmness there is something that unites them. It unites them across different experiences and different places, and even across different ages. That is why, of course (if you have read the chapter on the Trinity), the artist Giovanni Lanfranco assembled them all in the dome of Sant' Andrea della Valle. The saints belong together. They are a community, what the creed calls the *communion of saints*.

We talk about the Spirit being *Holy* and we note that what the Spirit does is turn us into community. When John V. Taylor wrote about the Spirit (in *The Go-Between God*), he suggested that the Spirit is the power and presence of God in the spaces between us, drawing us into relationship. Belief in Church, in forgiveness and in the communion of saints is belief in relationship. The language of salvation, reminding us that we are members of a body, and will share in the life of a city, and inhabit a kingdom, is the language of inclusion and relationship. Different from one another, we are yet made to be one in Christ. In Augustine's words,

> Marvel and rejoice we have become Christ. For if he is the head, we are the members; he and we together are the whole man . . .[3]

The saints of God, the saints in scripture and in history, were the people from down the road, from round here, who followed Christ closely enough for their lives to begin to look a bit like his. We should notice both their individuality and their common calling. We should notice that they so often come to us with place names attached – Hugh of Lincoln, Augustine of Canterbury, Richard of Chichester. We should notice the way they have been made patrons of places and individuals, notice the links forged with their particularity. Belief in this communion of saints is belief in a community of relationship and common life and it is a community unbreached by death. It is a belief that we belong in the community of the faithful that has lived the same life of Christ, shared in the same communion at the same common table, and died in the same hope.

It is into this same community that we are invited. Paul, writing his letters, addressed them to those 'called to be saints' in Rome and in Corinth, or to the 'saints' in Philippi. It is precisely this same business of being in the world and yet set apart for God and firm in that calling that marks out the Christian vocation. It has its focus in Christ who is supremely what holiness looks like and it is nurtured by holy things given to us in the sacraments. In the Byzantine rite of the Eucharist, the priest raises the host with the words, 'holy things for holy people'.

All those funerals, where we strive to hold the dead in remembrance and in company, should be a celebration of the company of the saints. We keep company with the saints and one another always. They came from our communities. They have gone before us and they assure us that by talking about the things we know, the things that have been, we are beginning to talk about the things that will be. The language for heaven is the language of this place, these people, the life we can describe.

This is John Donne, again:

> we do live together already, in a holy communion of saints, and shall live together for ever, hereafter, in a glorious resurrection of bodies . . . if the dead, and we, be not upon one floor, nor under one storey, yet we are under one roof.[4]

He knows that the dead are dead. He does not try to salvage them for us. Instead, he finds a place for them and for us in the company of the saints. These saints (and they may not necessarily have haloes, or possess a piece of paper proving their sanctity; the word is just shorthand for the people of God) summon us into giving an account of our future in which we don't make guesses in the dark, but speak of what we know. John Donne goes on:

> We think not a friend lost, because he is gone into another room, nor because he is gone into another land; and into another world, no man is gone; for that heaven, which God created, and this world, is all one world . . .
>
> This is the faith that sustains me, when I lose by the death of others, or when I suffer by living in misery myself, that the dead, and we, are now all in one church, and at the resurrection, shall be all in one choir.[5]

Notes

1 H. S. Holland, 'Death the King of Terrors', https://en.wikisource.org/wiki/The_King_of_Terrors (accessed 5 March 2019).

2 J. Donne, 'Death's Duel', sermon, 1630, available online at https://www.ccel.org/ccel/donne/deaths_duel.i.html.

3 Augustine, quoted in G. Chapman, *Catechism of the Catholic Church* (London: Continuum), p. 795.

4 J. Donne, Sermon XX, 1627, available online at https://www.biblestudytools.com/classics/the-works-of-john-donne-vol-1/sermon-xx.html.

5 Donne, Sermon XX.

16

All Souls

Surrender to the love of God

It was late afternoon but still broad daylight, outside one of Bristol's better hotels. I was late. If I had not been in a hurry, I might have stopped to take a longer look. I had, briefly, come face to face with the living dead. About 20 of them, plus, I think, two witches (one of them channelling *The Wizard of Oz*) and a vampire. They were posing for a picture. It struck me that the photographer had misunderstood the nature of the entertainment; he was asking them to *smile*. It was not Halloween, but Halloween was only four or five days away, so this close encounter with the undead was not in the least alarming. I walked on, in my cassock, wondering if anyone around assumed that I was part of this performance.

I am not keen on Halloween. It is not that I think Halloween is pagan, or dangerous (aside from a mild hesitation about unaccompanied children out at night, high on sugar). I do not accept the argument that Halloween is profoundly sinful. Sin, real sin, the kind that forms deadly habits, does not wear fancy dress. I have to own up: part of my problem with Halloween is just a curmudgeonly dislike of a brand that is packaged, promoted and sold that condemns me to public spaces festooned with faux cobwebs. More seriously, though, here is an annual conspiracy to persuade us that we do not need to take death seriously. It is all such a *game*. Death is not a party. We used to know that. The Bible considers death to be *unnatural*. We were not created to die. Death is the punishment meted out on Adam and Eve; it is the wages of sin. Previous generations feared death and kept it in mind. They would be puzzled that we make it frivolous.

Halloween is part of a sequence of days at the end of October and beginning of November that seems still to be a work in progress. It is a period that has Christians thinking about saints and about the faithful dead. It also includes a national memorial for the war dead and a carnival of ghouls, ghosts and things that go bump in the night. It was the saints that came first. More specifically, it began with the martyrs. Giving up their lives, as Christ had done, the martyrs were widely assumed to have gained the reward of resurrection. As a consequence, the common feast for martyrs was located in or near the Easter season. In baptism, every Christian enters into the mystery of Christ who died and rose again. We are all 'Easter people'. The martyrs, it was argued, have gone further. They have tasted both death and resurrection; their sanctity always points us to Easter. It was inevitable that their lives would be celebrated in that season. Gradually, though, the theological precision of this argument was lost and the feast of All Saints was shifted in the ninth century to 1 November. The memorial day of All Souls followed about 150 years later. That left us with a sequence of three holy days: All Saints' Day on 1 November (known as All Hallows), the vigil that fell before it, on 31 October (known as All Hallows' Eve), and All Souls' Day on 2 November.

Now, it is the first day, Halloween, historically the least interesting of the three, that steals the show. The Church, suddenly aware that it has lost the initiative and the plot, has responded with alternatives to Halloween, and struggles fitfully, and not very successfully, to shift the focus on to a reflection on light and dark. At the same time, and for different reasons, the Church has also developed a new and longer season of Remembrance-tide, taking in Remembrance Sunday and changing the meaning all over again. What began as a celebration of lives in which we glimpse a little Easter has become a more mournful reflection on mortality. The popular celebration of Halloween, meanwhile, is just a festival of the macabre, all make-up and make-believe.

Halloween is a pageant of the imagination. Remembrance Sunday, meanwhile (which is becoming increasingly popular and brings more people to church than it did), asks us to try to call to mind some very particular facts. These two days, so close together, juggle contradictory commitments. Halloween turns to fiction and film. Remembrance takes us to war memorials and rolls of honour. It directs us to trenches, beachheads and battle-fields. Books and television bombard us with detail, with indi-vidual acts of bravery and with specific moments of horror. It is done with the best of intention and with real skill. The trouble is that we usually sit in armchairs as we consume all this infor-mation. The philosopher and essayist George Steiner was surely right when he argued that *real* Remembrance is virtually impos-sible. We cannot remember, or even begin to imagine, what it was like on Omaha beach, or in Bergen-Belsen, or at Hiroshima.

Meanwhile, the two crucial days that fall between Halloween and Remembrance, the much more ancient feasts of All Saints (the commemoration of the people who were like us, but became defined by holiness) and All Souls (the commemoration of the ordinary lives of the faithful), struggle to command our attention. When we talk about the dead we get fanciful, or we get too specific. It is either Halloween, conjuring up images out of nowhere while hard evidence slips out of the door shaking its head, or it is Remembrance, when we pin all our confidence on our reverence for the past. It is either a fantasy or a back-ward glance. As a way of talking about death it is profoundly unsatisfactory.

Christian faith is an invitation to follow Christ. We are called to 'belong to Jesus Christ' (Romans 1.6). We long to grow to maturity in Christ; 'to the measure of the full stature of Christ' (Ephesians 4.13). Faith, therefore, begins with the life of Christ and insists on the specifics. Faith is rooted in history. It is fashioned out of objects with weight and shape: the wood of the cross, the nails, the stone rolled across the tomb. There really is an act of *remembrance* in our faith, which is repeated again and again in the Eucharist. Christian faith is rooted in history and the language it uses is all about real things. There is a steady insistence in the Gospels that Jesus was born when Augustus was emperor and was crucified under Pontius Pilate. We are given time and place and we can locate Christ's life, his death and his resurrection. When we talk about faith, when we talk about life, or death, we start with what we know.

It is odd that we keep forgetting what we have been told. Too quickly, we turn heaven into a place we can only approach through the imagination. In the Tate Gallery, there are three great panels painted by John Martin, each of them ten feet across. They offer an epic glimpse of what is to come. One of them is called *The Plains of Heaven*, and it is full of impossible and dreamy vistas. Martin completely ignores the fact that scripture uses a very different register. The Tate explains that Martin's picture recreates the vision of the Book of Revelation, 'a new heaven and a new earth' (Revelation 21.1–2). In truth, with his green fields and mountain vistas, he has painted something St John the Divine never imagined:

> Then I saw a new heaven and a new earth; for the first heaven and the first earth had passed away, and the sea was no more. And I saw the holy city, the new Jerusalem, coming down out of heaven . . . (Revelation 21.1–2)

Revelation looked for a renewed Jerusalem. It looked for a place it already knew. Enter that city and you would recognize the geography, be able to find your way round. Heaven is *not* an imaginary construct. Scripture keeps telling us that the future of the redeemed will be strangely familiar. It will be a community – a city, a kingdom, a house. The life everlasting is an eternity of relationship, and the language that describes it uses familiar images. We do not need fantastic imaginings, we already have a better language. Imagination will let us down. It will take us into the weird world of John Martin where the blessed float above a landscape that for all its beauty is strangely ethereal and *unreal*.

There are things that we know. Then, of course, there is a limit to what is known. Resurrection is only glimpsed, it is not yet *given*. The Gospels are laced with reminders that the bridegroom is still to come; the tenants and the servants look for the arrival of the landlord and master. 'Listen,' says St Paul, 'I will tell you a mystery! We will not all die, but we will all be changed' (1 Corinthians 15.51). The future remains mysterious. What is to come is only glimpsed. In the words of C. S. Lewis, what we have is

> the scent of a flower we have not found, the echo of a tune we have not heard, news from a country we have never yet visited.[1]

We live between the known and unknown, the now and the not yet. Imagination will sell us short and so will mere remembrance.

Death requires that we 'let go': not just that we let go of life, but that we let go of what we know. Eamon Duffy has written, 'death is that which undoes us, the nothing into which everything living falls'.[2] The Bible describes death as 'the last enemy'. It is the punishment for the sin of Adam (and thus 'the wages of sin'). As I have already explained, death confronts us with a gnawing sense of unfinished business. It is also sheer loss. Thinking about his own death, in *The Enduring Melody* Michael Mayne wrote:

> It's the sense of leaving behind all that is familiar and loved, the small delights as well as the larger joys, that causes us anguish if we are brought face-to-face with the sudden possibility of dying. It makes the deaths of those who have barely tasted life so particularly hard to bear.[3]

He concluded, in this book in which he had struggled with faith and death:

> We each choose to die in our own way, though for some it will be harder than for others, but if we can see it as 'gift', then it will be so insofar as we face it in such a way as to

draw good out of it; trying (however reluctantly, however painfully) to deliberately unseal our clenched fists and let go of what we have been given with open hands.[4]

We will never face death with equanimity until we accept that we must lose control. In 1946 C. S. Lewis published a short book describing an encounter with life after death. He called it *The Great Divorce*. Eager to give it a popular feel he filled it with turns of phrase that now seem a little dated. There are a few too many people in *The Great Divorce* saying 'By gum'. Persist, however, and there is some wonderful commentary on the way we struggle to let go. In one encounter, a great painter, standing in the foothills of the heavenly kingdom, wants to know if he can go on painting. An angelic figure wonders why he would want to do that:

'. . . isn't one going to be allowed to go on painting?'
'Looking comes first.'
'But I've had my look. I've seen just what I want to do. God! – I wish I'd thought of bringing my things with me!'
The Spirit shook his head, scattering light from his hair as he did so. 'That sort of thing's no good here,' he said.
'What do you mean?' said the Ghost.
'When you painted on earth – at least in your earlier days – it was because you caught glimpses of Heaven in the earthly landscape. The success of your painting was that it enabled others to see the glimpses too. But here you are having the thing itself. It is from here that the messages came. There is no good telling us about this country, for we see it already. In fact we see it better than you do.'[5]

What the angel tries to explain to the artist is that we must all learn to love something other than ourselves. Even artists need to stop loving their own artistry.

Every poet and musician and artist, but for Grace, is drawn away from love of the thing he tells, to love of the telling till, down in Deep Hell, they cannot be interested in God at all but only in what they say about Him. For it doesn't stop at being interested in paint, you know. They sink lower – become interested in their own personalities and then in nothing but their own reputations.[6]

Death is a surrender and it is a loss. It is the last loss of self that makes it possible to love something else, something that goes on for ever.

All Souls is not just an invitation to keep the dead in mind. This is the day when we assert that the one story of the living and the dead is an act of surrender to God. At All Souls we look for the fulfilment that is to come, the story that has yet to be told. At All Souls we acknowledge that it is a story that began before us and continues without us. We are swept up in the great purposes of God.

Notes

1 C. S. Lewis, *The Weight of Glory* (London: Macmillan, 1966), p. 5.

2 E. Duffy, *Creed in the Catechism: The Life of God for Us* (London: Geoffrey Chapman, 1996), p. 107.

3 M. Mayne, *The Enduring Melody* (London: Darton, Longman & Todd, 2006), p. 135.

4 Mayne, *The Enduring Melody*, p. 50.

5 C. S. Lewis, *The Great Divorce* (London: Fount, 1997), pp. 64–5.

6 Lewis, *The Great Divorce*, p. 65.

17

The Year of Grace

A Christian year?

If you listen to Radio 4's *I'm Sorry I Haven't A Clue*, you will be with familiar with the game 'one song to the tune of another'. It was the very first game, on the very first show. Panellists have to sing the lyrics of one song to the usually entirely unsuitable tune of another song. Tony Hawks singing The Smiths' 'Girlfriend in a Coma' to the tune of 'Tiptoe through the Tulips' is hard to forget.

You have picked up a book about the Christian year and (unless you are cheating and starting towards the back) you may already have begun to smell a rat. Surely, a book on the Christian year should have had more to say about the seasons. There have been some obvious omissions and some strange emphases. Ash Wednesday has had our attention, but what happened to Lent? There was a shameful neglect of the Sundays of Christmas, and of the Easter season. Worse still, the saints were unceremoniously swept up and tumbled together into All Saints. So, no Peter, no Paul, no Mary Magdalene. Just two feasts of the Blessed Virgin Mary – Candlemas and the Annunciation – had chapters to themselves. Admirers of Our Lady will feel cheated. What happened to the Visitation, the Conception, or her 'day' on 15 August? Where, come to that, was the Transfiguration, Corpus Christi, or Holy Cross Day? This has been a very selective survey of the Christian year.

Cards on the table: the book you are reading has been attentive to the Christian year, but it has been played out against a different tune. In fact, this book was something else *before* it was a book about the Christian year. This book is a commentary on the Apostles' Creed. Each of the chapters you have read has taken one festival, or one season, and matched that to one of the phrases of the creed. When you read about Christmas, you were reading about Jesus who was 'born of the Virgin Mary'. When you read about Ash Wednesday, you were reading about 'the forgiveness of sins'. The sequence of the chapters did follow the pattern of the Christian year, beginning in Advent, and moving through Christmas, to Epiphany, but all the time I had an eye on the creed. As a consequence, this was the creed as you have never said it, delivered in a strange and shuffled order. We did not come to the first clause, 'I believe in God, the Father almighty' until we got to Trinity. The book actually began right in the middle of the creed. In Advent, the Church has always looked to the last things and remembered that the Christ who comes to us at Christmas is also the one who 'will come to judge the living and the dead'.

The year and the creed have been linked like this:

I believe in God, the Father almighty,	Trinity
creator of heaven and earth.	Ordinary Time
I believe in Jesus Christ, his only Son, our Lord,	Epiphany
who was conceived by the Holy Spirit,	Annunciation
born of the Virgin Mary,	Christmas
suffered under Pontius Pilate,	Palm Sunday
was crucified . . .	Good Friday
died, and was buried; he descended to the dead.	Easter Eve
On the third day he rose again;	Easter
he ascended into heaven,	Ascension
he is seated at the right hand of the Father,	

and he will come to judge the living and the dead.	Advent
I believe in the Holy Spirit,	Pentecost
the holy catholic Church,	Candlemas
the communion of saints,	All Saints
the forgiveness of sins,	Ash Wednesday
the resurrection of the body,	All Souls
and the life everlasting.	

Or, if you like your year in order:

Advent	and he will come to judge the living and the dead.
Christmas	born of the Virgin Mary,
Epiphany	I believe in Jesus Christ, his only Son, our Lord,
Candlemas	the holy catholic Church,
Ash Wednesday	the forgiveness of sins,
Annunciation	who was conceived by the Holy Spirit,
Palm Sunday	suffered under Pontius Pilate,
Good Friday	was crucified . . .
Easter Eve	died, and was buried; he descended to the dead
Easter	On the third day he rose again;
Pentecost	I believe in the Holy Spirit,
Ascension	he ascended into heaven,
	he is seated at the right hand of the Father,
Trinity	I believe in God, the Father almighty,
Ordinary Time	creator of heaven and earth.

All Saints	the communion of saints,
All Souls	the resurrection of the body,
	and the life everlasting.

Salvation has come to this house

This link that I have made, between our faith and the liturgical seasons, is neither radical nor novel. Since ancient times we have named the days of the week after the gods and assumed that we live within a greater narrative. Our calendar of feasts, fasts and seasons has always been much more than a list of liturgical appointments. Admittedly, the rabbit holes of liturgical precision are all around. It is perfectly possible to do the detail and forget the view. I have had my moments of debating the right liturgical colour when it is the Second Sunday before Advent in the 'Kingdom' season, but the early morning service is from *The Book of Common Prayer* and the readings tell you that this is the Twenty-Fourth Sunday after Trinity. Too much of that and you will live a life sentence in the footnotes of faith.

Liturgy and the worship of the Church's year should always point beyond itself to the one we worship. This is a 'year of grace'. It is an invitation to make a journey into a more deeply understood belief. Each year, in a sequence of Sundays and seasons, we rehearse the life of Christ. We stop and pay attention to his birth, the arrival of the magi, his baptism, the entry into Jerusalem and so on. The year is a whole history of salvation. The feast days, the sequence of readings and prayers celebrate the work of the Spirit and proclaim the mystery of the Father. Observing the liturgical seasons, we set those truths in our midst and we impose that pattern on our daily lives. It is a point that was made movingly in *The Way of Christlikeness*, the last book Michael Perham wrote. He began by describing the death of his own father, which took place during one Holy Week. That year, Michael shuttled between services in his church and his father's deathbed. He was there on Good Friday; he gave his father communion, for the last time, on Easter Day.

> You cannot, I believe, move from the liturgy to these 'real life' experiences without making connections, without seeing that in the experience of Christ is the experience of every person . . . We keep Holy Week to make us open, sensitive and faithful in all the testing experiences of human life, to help us make connections in all of them.[1]

The Christian year is doctrine; it teaches us the faith. It is not a routine, or a calendar; it is a challenge. With dreadful symmetry, Michael's own health collapsed in Holy Week. The last conversation I had with him was on Good Friday. We talked about the fact that priests have to learn to let go. There is a temptation, in a ministry of preaching and teaching, that can have us believing our own publicity. A ministry like Michael's, so confident and compelling in leading us to encounter God in worship, might persuade us that we know how to name the living God, that we can navigate a path into his presence. In truth, we must all come to the place and the time when we must acknowledge that the glory and holiness of God eludes the best we can say and do. Real faith is never possession, it is always surrender. As the medieval theologian and mystic Meister Eckhart explains, we have to take leave of God:

> The noblest and the ultimate thing that a person can forsake is that he forsakes God for God's sake. Now St Paul forsook God for God's sake; he left everything that he was able to take from God and left everything that God was able to give him and everything that he was able to receive from God. When he had left all this, he left God for God's sake, and there remained for him.[2]

We have to let go of what we thought we knew. I made that point to Michael with particular conviction on Good Friday, having come from the cathedral where the Three Hours had ended in silence at the foot of a cross. Our worship, our paying attention to the seasons, helps us to escape ourselves and all we think we know.

David Stancliffe, a former Chair of the Church of England's Liturgical Commission, in a breezy and brilliant short essay, argues that some of our worship is not so much intended to change us but rather to draw attention to the one who comes among us. Other worship, however, is very definitely 'a rehearsal of change':

> 'Once you were no people but now you are God's people' (1 Peter 2.10) . . . Above all, it is true of the Eucharist, where the scattered company of wayward individuals is yet again being made one in the Body of Christ.[3]

Worship and the calendar of worship does not just inform us, it changes us. We are drawn away from what we know and into the life of Christ. This is the liturgical scholar, Philip Pfatteicher:

> The Church's year is not simply a calendar of festivals and seasons to remind us of the basics of the faith. It is in fact none other than the Lord of the Church living in his people, walking with them in their pilgrimage through this world. The seasons and feasts of the liturgical year unfold step by step the mystery of Christ from his coming into the world, to his passion, death, and resurrection, to his promised return in glory.[4]

Each and every Sunday is 'the Lord's Day', a weekly proclamation of the resurrection and a glimpse of a new creation. The whole year, all of our Christian calendar, is a rehearsal of God's glory and the story of his life among us. Every time we step into church we step into that story. We may well arrive full of our own drama and desire, worried about work, or a relative, wondering if we have left the oven on, incensed about something in the news, depressed perhaps, or elated. We bring all that with us, and so do the people around us. We can, of course, go home feeling just as preoccupied as we were, but if we will allow it, all that jumble of experience and desire can be gathered into the life of God. We can escape preoccupation and find our place in something more.

This may be beginning to sound suspiciously pious. Transformation and change do not come easily. I have been in church nursing my own concerns and holding them tight often enough to know that I cannot *expect* to encounter something else. I cannot anticipate or require a glimpse of God's loving purpose. 'Today salvation has come to this house,' said Jesus (Luke 19.9), but he said it in the house of Zacchaeus the tax collector, and most people did not see and did not believe. Living within the routines of the Christian year can point you beyond yourself, but the greedy self will fight back. Jesus preached out of a burning certainty that *this moment* is defining, for here and now the kingdom comes close and this is *the day of the Lord*. He died in that belief decried precisely by people of faith.

It's like going to the theatre or the cinema. We are perfectly capable of sitting through a good film or play unmoved, irritated by the person blocking our view, or preoccupied with some dilemma we carried into the theatre with us. We do better when we are lifted out of our own experience and begin to think about something fresh and unfamiliar. We do best of all when the drama carries on its work in us and changes us. For that to happen it has to be a good play or film, and we have to be willing participants.

We are no longer our own property

This year of faith evolved in the northern hemisphere. It is no accident that it ends as the days get shorter, and after the leaves have fallen from the trees. We have long been familiar with the idea that Christmas and Epiphany are *winter* feasts. Thanks to Lancelot Andrewes (and later T. S. Eliot), we are routinely reminded that the magi made a 'cold' journey and arrived in 'dead of winter'. Robert Southwell's Christmas poem 'The Burning Babe' begins on a 'hoary winter's night'. The presiding idea here is that the miracle of Christmas, the birth of life itself, looks all the more unlikely for occurring at 'the worst time of the year'. We have been told this often enough, and we are reminded every time we sing 'In the bleak midwinter' or 'See amid the winter's snow'. We are, perhaps, a bit less familiar with the way other connections have been made as seasons chime with liturgical routines. An Orthodox hymn, for example, reflects on Lent and makes a connection with the new season:

> The springtime of the Fast has dawned
> The flower of repentance has begun to open.[5]

Gerard Manley Hopkins made a similar point in 'May Magnificat':

> May is Mary's month . . .

> All things rising, all things sizing
> Mary sees, sympathizing
> With that world of good
> Mary's motherhood.

Much later, the last few weeks of the old year bring us into a season of remembrance and to All Souls. As nature shuts down around us, we come to the knowledge that our desires will end and that we will lose control and lose possession. We reach our limits at the end of the year. If you attend a church that keeps the Feast of Christ the King that point is made particularly clearly. Instituted in 1925, the observation of Christ the King was first fixed for the last Sunday of October. That caused convinced Protestants to raise a godly eyebrow because that Sunday is also Reformation Sunday. In 1970, the Second Vatican Council shifted the observance to the very last Sunday of the liturgical year, the Sunday before Advent. Subsequently it became more popular and found its way into other church calendars. Pope Pius XI, who gave us this feast of Christ the King, had some rather particular local and political ambitions in mind. He wanted to say something about true kingship to fascists and Bolsheviks, who cared about such things, and also say it to a cocktail generation that did not care a bit. Setting out his stall, however, the Pope quoted Cyril of Alexandria, and made a rather broader point:

> Christ has dominion over all creatures, a dominion not seized by violence nor usurped, but his by essence and by nature . . . We are no longer our own property, for Christ has purchased us with a great price; our very bodies are the members of Christ.[6]

We are no longer our own property. In the course of the year, something is happening *around* us, something we do not control, and something is happening *to* us. However much we would like to think that the liturgical year is something we have made and that we keep (in the way we talk about *keeping* Christmas), the truth is that the year takes charge.

Our Christian year is so much more than a routine of observance, or a religious duty. The observance, it is true, can loom pretty large. We may be very conscious of the fact that we have made an effort to tip up in church, collect a hymn book (and perhaps a palm cross on Palm Sunday, or a candle at Candlemas). We can be acutely self-conscious walking down the street behind a donkey. We can notice that we are saying and doing certain things that seem, frankly, *odd*. We can notice our own effort and our attentiveness. Noticing that, however, we are distracted. Our year of faith is the declaration of what God has done and what God is doing now. Not us, but *God*. It is the life of Christ that we encounter in church, the life of Christ that is described in liturgy and sermon. This Christian year is not of our doing, not of our making; it is a gift. It really is a year of a grace; a thing we have not earned. Faith is never an extra activity for us (everyday life plus, for the holy few, prayers, scripture, and studied acts of kindness). Nor is faith a decision, or an extra capacity, like deciding to support Tranmere Rovers, or learning Flemish. Faith is never an addition, nor an acquirement. Faith is fundamentally a *gift*. You accept it, or you don't. If you accept it, it changes you, not necessarily very quickly and not all at once. It changes you for life. It changes us so that we can live life fully.

So, alongside the calendar I keep in the kitchen, the one that marks out birthdays, holidays, appointments and anniversaries, I have another set of engagements in a lectionary on my desk: Christmas, Lent, Holy Week and Easter. Both calendars record the consequence of commitments I have made. I have agreed to meet a friend for lunch, I have said I will go to a meeting, I have promised to take the cat to the vet. The Christian calendar works in exactly the same way, but of course it is less provisional (the cat escaped once and we did not get to the vet). God's action is sure; salvation does not fail. Both calendars have things to say about the future. The kitchen calendar records commitments that might be familiar or challenging (you will have gathered that the cat really does not like going to the vet) and they are unscripted. The lectionary provides some familiarity (I know roughly what Christmas will be like, we did it last year and the year before) and yet there is unpredictability here too. As I step into my own future, and into God's future, I will be changed. I can hedge against danger, I can take precautions, but I cannot manage the future. 'Pass the tambourine', wrote the poet Kathleen Jamie, as she reminded us that God is a God 'of movement',[7] while Louis MacNeice told us that the world is 'crazier and more of it than we think'.

> World is crazier and more of it than we think,
> Incorrigibly plural. I peel and portion
> A tangerine and spit the pips and feel
> The drunkenness of things being various.[8]

The words 'vet' or 'Fifteenth Sunday after Trinity' in my calendars can only hint at the range of possibilities that lie ahead.

Looking to these commitments, I have to use my imagination; here is what I will become. Using the lectionary, I have the creed to help me think through exactly what my commitment might mean. The calendar invites me into faith and the creed is a commentary on what the calendar foretells. Calendars require an act of faith. The commitment and the faith need putting into words.

Notes

1 M. Perham, *The Way of Christ-likeness* (Norwich: Canterbury Press, 2016), p. 6.

2 Meister Eckhart, 'Sermon 12 *Qui audit me*' in B. McGinn (ed.), *Meister Eckhart* (New York: Paulist Press, 1968), p. 268.

3 D. Stancliffe, 'Is there an Anglican Liturgical Style?' in K. Stevenson and B. Spinks (eds), *The Identity of Anglican Worship* (London: Mowbray, 1991), p. 127.

4 P. Pfatteicher, *Journey into the Heart of God: Living the Liturgical Year* (Oxford: Oxford University Press, 2013), p. 345.

5 From the Vespers in the week before Lent.

6 *The Encyclical*, Quas Primas 13.

7 K. Jamie, 'The Way We Live' in *Mr and Mrs Scotland are Dead: Poems 1980–1994* (Hexham: Bloodaxe Books, 2002).

8 L. MacNeice, 'Snow' in *Collected Poems* (London: Faber, 1966), p. 30.

18

Believing in the Church

I believe

The Apostles' Creed is familiar if you work in a cathedral. We say it daily, at evensong. If, like most of us, you usually go to church on Sundays, you are more likely to know the longer, Nicene Creed, the one that begins:

> We believe in one God,
> The Father, the Almighty,
> Maker of heaven and earth,
> Of all that is,
> Seen and unseen

The Nicene Creed has been included in our services since the end of the fifth century, but it took shape even earlier. Something very like it has been tugging at our sleeve, telling us 'this is how it is' since the days of the Emperor Constantine. This creed emerged out of a Church full of debate and disagreement. We have this creed because that bitter argument had to be contained. That means that the Nicene Creed comes at you wagging a finger. It tells you, 'You can say this and you must not say something else.' When we say this creed we are rehearsing an argument that was important and decisive, but one we would not now put into the same words in the same way. The Nicene Creed is a reverent, backward glance at our history as well as an affirmation of historic faith.

The Apostles' Creed is a different thing. It dates from the end of the fourth century, although again parts of it were being used at baptisms much earlier than that. It is wrapped up now inside all the genteel dignity that Choral Evensong can muster and we can miss a little of the urgency within it. Being shorter than the Nicene Creed, there is much less careful qualification in the text. Consequently, the Apostles' Creed feels complete and final. Indeed, reading the commentaries that have been written about it, the Apostles' Creed often turns into something to be received and admired. Scholars who write about our worship tell us that the Apostles' Creed could now be seen as the 'climax' to the ministry of the word, or as a kind of 'response' to the sermon.[1] That is not where we started, however, and it does the creed a bit of a disservice. This creed had its beginning in a commitment, a life choice. This creed was once electric. It was a pledge of new commitment and a statement of new intention. Saying these words was a turning point, a commitment to something fresh and startling. We can far too easily miss the fizz and bounce of this creed. Years ago, I read a children's novel, *The Wind Eye*, by Robert Westall. It is set on Lindisfarne and St Cuthbert looms large within it. Early in the novel, there is a wonderful aside about the way Christianity can change with the passing years.

> It was marvellous and dangerous at the start, but people keep making it safer all the time. I mean, the Wright brothers could see the ground ripping past and feel the wind in their hair, but now it's all jumbo jets and bad movies. The *old* Christians felt the wind in their hair.[2]

It is that sense we need to recover as we pick up the Apostles' Creed. This is the faith into which Christians were baptized and it was shocking. Joseph Martos writes:

> And what did baptism mean? One thing that is clear is that baptism marked a dividing line between the old and the new, between waiting for the messiah and finding him, between living with guilt and living with forgiveness, between being in a community of law and being in a community of forgiveness.[3]

Here were the words that would describe a new way of life.

Anxious, for good pastoral reasons, that the words of the creed might seem puzzling or opaque, clergy and others can too quickly surround it with qualification and commentary. We temper the demands the words make on us. We produce careful explanations of clauses like 'conceived by the Holy Spirit', 'descended to the dead'. Thus, in quick, short steps, we begin to reassure ourselves that while the creed is important, it is not perhaps quite *decisive*.

> A creed is not, and was never meant to be, a substitute for personal faith; it attempts to give substance to a personal faith that already exists. You do not become a Christian by reciting a creed . . .
>
> Some of the components of the creed may seem a little strange or unfamiliar if you have come to faith only recently. Don't be alarmed by this: it is just a gentle reminder that there is more to Christianity than you think at this stage.[4]

Here Alister McGrath has got this right (of course he has). He knows that there *is* a demand here and that there is more to Christianity than we might think. Even so, he could be heard to suggest that there is 'personal faith' and *then* there are creeds. That could suggest a distinction between an experience and commitment I treasure, and the words I must use in a service, for which the Church later provides a set of notes. While I do not think that is what he means, this is a real temptation for Christians. Remembering a moment of conversion, and the change it made for us, we start talking about 'my' faith. Faith then turns into a possession. What we feel and what we think are crucial to us, but they are really not where we start. Putting personal faith before the creed gets things precisely the wrong way round. The Apostles' Creed, with its roots in the rite of baptism, was never a commentary on a decision we had made. You can drive a car without knowing how the engine works and what words to use to describe what you find under the bonnet. You cannot, though, be a Christian without being able to put that faith into words. Faith is always a summons. This creed is a statement made about moving from *here* to *there*. We do not make a life choice that later involves us in saying the creed. The creed describes the experience we are called into and the life we must live. The experience properly *follows* the commitment. Saying the creed, then, is an act of trust.

Exploring the same idea in slightly different language, Rowan Williams makes the point that we have grown used to a culture of suspicion. Trust is not something we give lightly. That makes creeds challenging. It is much more comfortable to treat creeds as a set of propositions we might debate (reserving our position about our personal faith). Making a commitment to something that feels a stretch is uncomfortable. That, though, is what creeds ask us to do.

> 'I believe in God the Father almighty' isn't the first in a set of answers to the question, 'How many ideas or pictures have I inside my head?' As if God were the name of one more doubtful thing like UFOs, or ghosts, to add to the list of the furniture of my imagination. It is the beginning of a series of statements about where I find the anchorage of my life, where I find solid ground, home.[5]

So, Rowan Williams can argue that to say the Apostles' Creed is to make a statement about where I belong.

We believe

In 1981, the Doctrine Commission of the Church of England produced a report called *Believing in the Church*. In his Introduction to this document, John V. Taylor, then Bishop of Winchester, began with a substantial quotation from a play by Dorothy L. Sayers. *The Just Vengeance* was written in 1946. The play reads rather oddly now (I tried it and failed to finish). Sayers imagines an airman, killed in World War Two, arriving at 'the city'. Clearly, we are meant to begin to imagine heaven, but interestingly what the airman sees is familiar. In fact, he recognizes this city as his native Lichfield; he has come home. The key question now is whether he truly belongs to this city, whether he can stay. The airman meets an angel, known as the Recorder, who asks him what is his claim to citizenship. The airman is young (he is also haunted by guilt from the violence of the war), and he confesses he has not achieved very much:

Recorder	What matters here is not so much what you did As why you did it . . . Can you recite your creed?
Airman	I believe in God . . .
Chorus	*(picking him up and carrying him along with it)* . . . the Father Almighty, Maker of heaven and earth. And in Jesus Christ . . .
Airman	No! No! No! What made me start off like that? I reacted automatically to the word 'creed'. My personal creed is something totally different.
Recorder	What is speaking in you is the voice of the city, The Church and household of Christ, Your people and your country, From whom you derive. Did you think you were unbegotten? Unfranchised? With no community and no past? Out of the darkness of your unconscious memory The stones of the city are crying out. Go on.[6]

It is a very literary exchange, but Sayers is on to something. She is trying to help us see that faith belongs to the Church. In the chapter on All Saints, I explained that when the Bible talks about our salvation and about heaven, the language is always corporate. We are the body of Christ and it has many members. We are called into a kingdom, we are to live in a city; we are invited to the heavenly feast. We are all saved together or we are not saved at all. In the Gospel of St John, we are shown that Jesus' great prayer, the prayer made the night before he died, was that we might be united,

> that they may all be one. As you, Father, are in me and I am in you, may they also be in us, so that the world may believe that you have sent me. (John 17.21)

So, Sayers' airman, however hard he tries to say something deeply personal, begins to speak with the voice of the Church. What he does is to recite the creed and as he does it the voice of the Church takes over. We say the creed hoping to inhabit it.

At the very beginning, in those early statements at baptism, the Apostles' Creed was simply an affirmation of things that really must be said about believing in the Father and the Son and the Holy Spirit. These are claims about the way things are, statements about our origins and our destination. Later, as the text was revised and reconsidered, phrases were added with a slightly different intent. It was becoming clear that there were things that really must be said and other things we should be careful *not* to say. So, for example, the creed is clear that God is creator of 'heaven and earth'. We are supposed to notice that this means that God creates *all* things. There must be no suggestion that God is not the creator of things we find difficult or unpleasant, like mosquitoes, the mycobacterium tuberculosis, or celery (I really do not like celery). The creed, then, contained teaching that was known to be true as well as teaching that we needed to receive. These are the gifts of God's grace and things we learn to accept. So, we do not say the creed because it is important that we all join in at a particular point in the service with a kind of 'hurrah for the gospel'. We say the creed because we need to recollect and recite what is God's gift to us. As Eamon Duffy puts it,

> Belief in God arises not from our search for God, but from God's loving search for us. Faith, the human response to the God who reveals and gives himself to us, is itself the free gift of God.[7]

God comes looking for us; God never depends on us to seek and find God. It is always God's initiative, never ours. The creed provides the language we need to receive this gift. It is language that we all use. The creeds are precisely not *personal* statements of belief. This is public utterance. This is what we say because we belong to a community that knows these things are true. Here is Duffy again, quoting the *Catechism of the Catholic Church*:

> 'no one can believe alone, just as no one can live alone'. To believe in God is to receive the good news from others and to share it in our turn. Individual Christians take their place in a 'great chain of believers'.[8]

The creed of the Apostles?

This is the language that the Church has agreed is always true, for everyone, everywhere. That is the reason the Church claims that this is the creed of the *Apostles*. The claim here is that this is eternal language and that it has been used by those who knew Christ and followed him. Just to be clear, however, the Apostles did not write the Apostles' Creed. There is a lively myth that it is, indeed, all their own work. That idea was already familiar as early as the fourth century. It is not difficult to track down quite ancient images that associate a particular apostle with a particular clause in the creed. That connection was then repeated over and over again. Go to churches where medieval art survives and you might well find evidence of this. At Mattishall in Norfolk, for example, St James is linked to the phrase 'who was conceived by the Holy Ghost, born of the Virgin Mary'. It is an attractive idea, but it is not true. It is a myth and in the way myths work, it has a purpose. The point is that this is a faith expressed in language that is apostolic, authoritative and always binding. It is a way of telling us that we can trust this language. An apostle technically is an *emissary* and the creed is the *embassy* of God, sent and given. No wonder we claim the Apostles wrote it.

Here is the language of faith. Here are the words that describe the experience of living in years of grace. This language helps us all to find a place in a Church that is apostolic; it expresses a commitment in which we live.

Believing in the Church

The temptation is to take this faith and try to make it *mine*. There is always a temptation to make faith *mine*. It is the temptation to which the Pharisees succumbed. Deeply religious people, living through a crisis of faith in a land given by God yet occupied by Romans, looking to a temple that they had thought touched heaven but now saw as compromised by the time-serving Herod and his cronies, the Pharisees wondered how to believe. The public landmarks of faith had fallen. So they asked, 'What now must I do?' They found an answer in imposing on themselves a staggering obligation. They would know themselves to be truly Jews by their obedience to the Law (the one thing that was undeniably and authentically Jewish). Their determination and dedication commands respect. The Pharisees' one failing, however, was not to notice that they had created a demand they could define. It was a huge demand, but it was law and it could be known. Matthew, Mark and Luke recount the story of the man who asked Jesus, 'Teacher, what good deed must I do to have eternal life?' (Matthew 19.16).

And he said to him, 'Why do you ask me about what is good? There is only one who is good. If you wish to enter into life, keep the commandments.' (Matthew 19.17)

Jesus begins this conversation with a statement that shakes the foundations. The man wants an answer he can manage – 'what good deed must I do?' He wants to know what is good. Jesus tells him that he does not know what he asks. What is good is too hard a question because goodness belongs to God. There follows a brief exchange about which commandments need to be kept.

He said to him, 'Which ones?' And Jesus said, 'You shall not murder; You shall not commit adultery; You shall not steal; You shall not bear false witness; Honour your father and mother; also, You shall love your neighbour as yourself.' The young man said to him, 'I have kept all these; what do I still lack?' Jesus said to him, 'If you wish to be perfect, go, sell your possessions, and give the money to the poor, and you will have treasure in heaven; then come, follow me.' (Matthew 19.18–21)

The man gets what he asked for, a description of what the Law requires. He gets much more than he asked for: 'go, sell your possessions . . . then come, follow me.' Faith is never something that we can contain, control or define. It is a gift of God, remember, an invitation, a summons into the life of Christ. That is why faith is always the language of the Church; language we agree together. It can never be merely *personal*. Faith is not what I think, faith is what I am given, and the place, the only place I can be given it, is in the body of Christ, in the Church. The Church is not a group of people who have decided what they believe and then agree to say their prayers together. The Church is the community that is being drawn closer to Christ. The worship of the Church teaches and guides us into the faith that the Church believes. Hearing the Scriptures read and listening to sermons is part of that, of course, but it goes much deeper. In Communion services, very different people, with very different concerns, set aside all their difference and do one thing together; they become one body. In the Christian year, through Christmas, Lent and Passiontide, we tell the story of Christ's life. These festivals are not just a commemoration, they make present what is always true. It was true then, and it is true for us now. So, for example, if you sing a well-known Christmas carol you will pray:

> O holy Child of Bethlehem,
> descend to us, we pray;
> cast out our sin, and enter in,
> be born in us today.[9]

A year in church *is* a journey into the faith. The cycle of readings and the rhythm of festivals is not devised to guide us through the creed (though there are those who argue that the whole year was once intended to teach the whole faith). We do not believe so that we can take part, we take part so that we might believe.

As Alister McGrath explains, a creed is the voice of the community.

> To become a Christian is to enter a community of faith whose existence stretches right back to the upper room in which Jesus met with his disciples.[10]

The community acknowledges a faith that reaches through time, back to the Apostles.

Not only does faith need to be put into words we can all use and trust, everywhere. It has to be *all* the faith. The community has always said that the faith is whole. It is this *and* that. It is Father, Son *and* Spirit. It is creation, death *and* resurrection. It is Church *and* the communion of saints. We cannot specialize, or settle for less. We accept that this faith we are given makes demands on us, asks us to grow in understanding and in the generosity of our comprehension. We receive the creed more than we possess it. This is the voice of the Church.

We speak the words and we let the voice of the Church take over.

I have made that point a number of times. I have explained to others, struggling with some phrase in the creed, that we are making a statement about what the Church believes in the hope that we can enter into that faith and into Christ's life in the Church more deeply. Only very recently, however, have I completely taken to heart what I was talking about.

While I was writing this book, my mother died. In her last years she was diminished, disoriented and often thoroughly miserable (though she was wonderfully well cared for). Dementia took not just her memory but significant parts of her speech. Conversation between us became more and more corrupted. As a result, a significant conversation between us was never completed. As a young woman, my mother had had a lively faith. In our house were some of the religious books that she had bought and read long before. C. S. Lewis was there, I remember: *The Four Loves* and *Screwtape*. Then, her own mother contracted cancer and died. This was before I was born and it was a bereavement that was not much discussed as I grew up. It was unspoken, and it was to some extent undigested. In Michael Rosen's wonderful phrase, my mother was 'carrying the elephant'. Her faith collapsed in the certainty that her mother was gone and could not be found. There was, in my mother's world, no hope of any life to come. The dead were dead. The religious books never came off the shelves. I grew up in a house where church was never mentioned. We did not even go to Christmas carol services.

When I finally made my own way to church, my mother followed me, hesitantly, a year or two later. She had a clear sense of what she had once had and lost; she hoped to recover something. She never gave up on that. She went fitfully to church for the next 40 years, but (with the possible exception of that last curious year when she seemed to enjoy the services arranged in the care home) she was never at ease with faith. She could not believe in the resurrection. We talked about that now and again, but the conversations never went well. None of my explanations helped. If anything, I just made matters worse. It seemed that all I could do was to demonstrate that there was a fundamental disagreement between us. We settled into an uneasy silence on the subject. The silence was still there when my mother died.

So, my mother's funeral looked difficult in prospect. She was quite small, just five foot two, but with the light of battle in her eyes she seemed bigger and possessed of a staggering gift for stubborn resistance. In life I had never been able to dismiss her opinions. I was not about to do that in death. I could not make claims for her that she would have struggled to accept. I hesitated about what we could say. Because I work in a cathedral, that is where the funeral was held, amid all that confident, soaring stone. That was statement enough. I certainly did not want to imply that 'She did not really believe this, but all of us here this morning know better.' In the event, a colleague took the funeral and I preached. I talked about her struggle to believe and I tried to avoid wishing my certainties upon her. Then I sat down, and suddenly the liturgy did the rest. My difficulty and my anxiety was swept away. It was not my voice, nor was it my mother's voice. This was not the old stalemate that had existed between us. This was the voice of the Church praying for her and declaring the hope that the Church has for those who have died. *We believe in the resurrection of the dead.*

The voice of the Church is there for me when my own voice is uncertain. The Church says things I might struggle to say. The voice of the Church is also there when I am not sure how much, or how little, I should say. I have already observed that theology, talking about God, can be difficult. It can be difficult because it is profound and a bit hard to grasp in its size and sweep. Most doctrine, in fact, is a lot simpler than it is made to sound. It usually only gets difficult when it is not explained very well. Even so, talking about God can be challenging because we are not sure when to start and when to stop. Sometimes we say too little, because we are bashful. More often, we say rather too much. Knowing something about Jesus and quite a lot about scripture we can forget that we have not begun to comprehend the true glory and holiness of God. Having a creed can give us some confidence. Here are some things that we *should* say. That is indeed what the Church believes. We have a creed, in part, to help us know what to say. It is worth pointing out at this stage that the Apostles' Creed is very short. If these are the things we can say, one conclusion might be that we should try not to say too much.

What we must say is that this is the language for all of us to use, all of the time everywhere. This is the language the Church has for God. We might learn this language (I really think we should) but it will never be my *first* language; this will always be the vocabulary for what lies ahead.

Notes

1 P. Bradshaw, *Companion to Common Worship* (London: SPCK, 2001), pp. 66–7; M. Perham, *New Handbook of Pastoral Liturgy* (London: SPCK, 2000), p. 122.

2 R. Westall, *The Wind Eye* (London: Catnip Publishing, 2007), p. 45.

3 J. Martos, *Doors to the Sacred* (Norwich: SCM Press, 1981), p. 165.

4 A. McGrath, *I Believe: Exploring the Apostles' Creed* (London: IVP, 1997), p. 15.

5 R. Williams, *Tokens of Trust: An Introduction to Christian Belief* (Norwich: Canterbury Press, 2007), p. 6.

6 D. Sayers, *The Just Vengeance* quoted in *Believing in the Church: The Corporate Nature of Faith* (London: SPCK, 1981), p. 1.

7 E. Duffy, *The Creed in the Catechism* (London: Geoffrey Chapman, 1996), p. 2.

8 Duffy, *Creed in the Catechism*, pp. 4–5.

9 Phillips Brooks, 'O little town of Bethlehem'.

10 McGrath, *I Believe*, p. 16.

19

Telling the Story

You will now be familiar with the idea that, like Dorothy L. Sayers' airman, we are tempted to make faith personal, make it *mine*. We want to possess our faith, manage it, and have it under our control. The trouble is, the more we do that the more we lose sight of the fact that faith is an invitation to change. Jesus said, 'Follow me'. He did not say, 'Follow your instincts'. He asked us to live our lives as he lived life, fully, and without making life a performance.

Faith is also a summons to community. We are saved together, or not at all. When the Epistle to the Ephesians imagines our vocation, it imagines what we will be together, imagines the virtues that allow us to flourish *together*,

> with all humility and gentleness, with patience, bearing with one another in love, making every effort to maintain the unity of the Spirit in the bond of peace. (Ephesians 4.2–3)

Growing into Christ is to grow in love (Ephesians 4.16), to be 'rooted and grounded in love' (Ephesians 3.17). That sounds lovely. In reality, it is far from straightforward. What Ephesians is trying to tell us, in urging us to be rooted and grounded in love, is that love must be the only and exclusive character of our lives. Love and nothing else. That is a condition we struggle to fulfil. Herbert McCabe has argued that the making of a perfect human being is the making of a new kind of relationship. Jesus is perfectly human because he lives a life 'unmixed with domination or exclusiveness'.[1] We should note that McCabe thinks it a *new* relationship. Instinctively love gets mixed with power, or need. To live in love is to begin anew. To live in love is to recognize that relationship is essential and defining.

Faith is never mine, it is always *ours*, and the creed is at pains to spell that out. I explained in the previous chapter that there used to be an idea that there are 12 clauses of the creed and that each clause was allocated to one of the Apostles. The truth is that there are really *three* clauses in the creed. We repeat the critical 'I believe' three times. I believe in God, the Father almighty . . . I believe in Jesus Christ . . . and I believe in the Holy Spirit. There are three essential statements to be made: that God creates, that God is seen in the life of Christ, and that God sustains our life as a *relationship*. Here is Nicholas Lash:

> There are three ways that we believe in God, ways which find expression in the three articles of the Creed. To be more exact: there are three ways in God, three ways God is . . .[2]

Lash suggests that the three clauses of the creed remind us that God is Father, the creator (Lash talks about *producing*). God is Son, the God born among us, living, dying and rising again (he calls that *appearing*). Then, God is Spirit, the life we live together with God and one another (which Lash calls *peace making*). When we say that we believe in one God, Father, Son and Spirit, one of the things we are saying is that relationship matters. We are asserting a relationship between the persons of the Trinity and reminding ourselves that faith requires relationship. As soon as we have said that we believe in God as Spirit, we are plunged into belief in the Church, in communion and in forgiveness. To believe at all is to believe together; to believe is to believe in community.

To hear us talk about our 'personal faith', however, is to hear us talk about ourselves. The world is full of the sound of us talking, and all too often we are talking to ourselves, and about ourselves. It is the great temptation. Writing about prayer, C. S. Lewis had his devil, Screwtape, lay out the strategy that would misdirect our best efforts:

Whenever they are attending to the Enemy [God] himself we are defeated, but there are ways of preventing them from doing so. The simplest is to turn their gaze away from him to themselves.[3]

When he wrote about hell Lewis described it as the place where humanity has utterly broken down, each person living in deeper and deeper isolation moving further and further away from any neighbour. The great commandments are to 'love God and love your neighbour as yourself'; that turns our gaze outward. Our greedy self drags us back.

Preoccupied

On the night of 15 October 2011, a small group of tents were pitched on College Green in Bristol. The following morning, a Sunday, I met some of the campers. In a sense, I knew who they were, as I had been tipped off that an Occupy protest was imminent. The sun was shining, they were outgoing and eager, we had a quick and cheerful conversation. I was rather dressed up and had to explain that I had to be somewhere else and really quite soon. They were a little dressed down, after a night in the tents, and clear that they were not going anywhere soon. We laughed. I knew about Occupy; it had already made a name for itself. Occupy Wall Street had been established in New York's Zuccotti Park a month earlier. They used the catchphrase 'We are the 99%'. This, they said, was an act of solidarity with the vast majority and an act of defiance against the 1% who owned a disproportionate amount of wealth and wielded a disproportionate political influence. Here was a witness against them, spirited, passionate, informed, and more than willing to talk. I had to be a little careful in what I said that morning, but in principle I agreed with them.

College Green gets its name from the college of Augustinian Canons who once lived around the abbey church to the south. It is, in fact, the site of their medieval graveyard. That abbey became Bristol Cathedral in 1542. After World War Two, a great sweep of offices and a debating chamber were built for the city council on the north side of The Green. At the same time, the railed, tree-lined paths were replaced with a flat expanse of grass (it was never the intention, but it created a good campsite). This is the civic centre of the city, owned by the cathedral but leased to the city council. The tents arrived because it was an obvious place for a protest. In mid-October, in the sunshine, none of us understood, or began to imagine, the legal and moral challenges ahead. It did not enter our heads that these few tents, one of a number of occupations that day, would become the second largest Occupy protest in the country (the camp at St Paul's Cathedral was bigger). We certainly never anticipated that tents would give way to wooden shanties, and that the protesters would hunker down through a long, cold winter. Occupy Bristol was only just beginning; it would continue until the morning of 31 January 2012.

In the autumn of 2011, I had been Dean of Bristol for about 18 months. I had never dealt with anything like this before. The Chapter, the governing body of the cathedral, was divided by the protest. Some of my colleagues wanted to sit on The Green in solidarity; one, I think, was wondering how to lay hands on a water cannon. Television, radio and newspapers besieged me, wanting to know what I thought. What I thought was that this was difficult and getting worse. As the days turned to weeks, the camp on our doorstep grew and changed. The Occupy movement deliberately made no demands. They did not want to be yet another group insisting on having their way, making one more grab for power. That was impressive, but the trouble is, if you have not decided what you are asking for you will never know when you have secured what you need. It was always going to be difficult to decide when the protest should end. The lack of focus also made the camp a safe haven for people with other agendas. Soon, we had to acknowledge that we had both a protest to deal with and, quite separately, an issue with a few people who were putting both themselves and us at risk.

Now, years later, I can tell this story and explain how we made decisions and how one thing followed another. At the time, however, I saw no pattern. The cast of characters kept changing; the situation felt volatile and unpredictable. In the midst of this story, there was no story. Things got worse, then they got better and then they would turn for the worse again. My colleagues were threatened and abused, members of the public complained to us that they had been attacked, and our services were occasionally disrupted. It felt occasionally fascinating, mainly worrying, and on a number of occasions quite frightening. We had conversations based around 'what if?' We did not have control of events; we certainly did not have a script. Some of that challenge was played out very publicly as I stood in front of a television camera. In all of that, what I remember most clearly is something personal. *My* anxiety, *my* uncertainty, *my* fear, that was what I knew. It was stressful. I did not sleep well. I found it difficult to pray.

Finding prayer difficult was a bleak experience. Admitting that prayer was difficult is uncomfortable. Prayer, surely, should be precisely the place you go at times like this. Patterns of prayer should turn out to be reliable and sure when you need them most. It was not like that for me. I could not cast all my care on the Lord; I failed miserably to find any reassurance that God was directing events. On every occasion that I tried to settle into silence, looking for the perspective that prayer can give, the sheer difficulty and enormity of my problems would rear up in front of me. I could not get past that. Sitting still and alone, I would suddenly feel even more isolated, and the mess and muddle of what I faced would fill my thoughts. It was a bit like trying to walk into the ocean to swim, only to find that the waves breaking on the beach keep pushing you back to where you started. I could not get over myself. The real horror of that was that I was alone with myself.

Fortunately, in a cathedral, there is plenty of prayer led by other people and there is a routine of the daily offices, Morning Prayer and evensong. When I went to those services, I could much more easily slot myself into the pattern they gave me.

I could pray those prayers. I could listen to the passages of scripture set for the day. In those services, I could pray for the people living in the camp, for my colleagues, for the council, and for myself. All the liturgies we prayed together and the steady movement, throughout the months of Occupy, that took us from All Saints and All Souls, into Advent, Christmas and then on to Epiphany, forced me into company. I was given other stories than my own; I shared other experiences. Left to myself, the experience I was living in was all-consuming. I could not escape myself; I had no words. The one thing that really helped me was another, different story; the steady reminder that my experience might not be king. To be clear, these services and the prayers within them did not resolve my difficulty. I was still lying awake at night. They did, however, shift my attention now and then. There were other things to think about. It did not all have to be about me.

A story with an unsatisfactory ending

Occupy kept me awake, and stopped me praying in silence, because in that silence this problem felt so very much *mine*. Occupy was *my* problem. It kept turning my eye inwards. To get any perspective at all I needed to start somewhere else, to think about something else.

Of course, I had a lot of advice, and support. I would have made terrible mistakes if I really had been all by myself. Part of my problem was an unbecoming tendency to wallow in self-pity. That said, I did also have a problem with some of my 'comforters'. I tried not to show it, but I was a bit impatient with people who told me it would 'soon be over', or that it would all 'turn out fine'. Like the prophets who declared 'peace, peace' when there was no peace, they did not convince. We had examined the options at length, we knew what the issues were, and it was quite clear that things might not be fine. There was a real danger that someone would get badly hurt. Reassurance did not feel reassuring.

A month or so into this strange season, I met a judge. Early in his career, he had spent long months in a bitterly contested inquiry, in the public eye (a much bigger news story than Occupy). He told me that if the protest on College Green ended well, then I would begin to see it differently. This was not a bland reassurance. I was well aware that he had said, '*If* this ends well you will understand it quite differently.' He talked about his experience of being in the midst of a storm and then the advantage of looking back at it when the noise and distraction died down. That judge offered me an ending. He suggested a possibility, a glimpse of a different future. When Occupy did finally end without serious casualties (at least, as far as I know) he was proved right. I had imagined all kinds of problems and seen some of them become a reality. However, when the shanties were dismantled, and grass finally grew again, the ending of the story shifted the meaning. I understood it differently. It did not help, *during* Occupy, to be told, 'It will all turn out fine'; that reassurance changed nothing. It was the ending that changed the meaning.

So, in that winter of discontent, I had some difficult lessons to learn. I made poor progress, but I did make progress. I learnt to accept help when it was offered (but I was still much too slow to go looking for all the help that was available). I also accepted that the prayers of the Church could carry me along when my own prayers failed. Those are lessons about 'getting over yourself'; not thinking it is all about me. Even coming to terms with that difficult truth, however, I still failed to put my trust in the future. I never got past living in the midst of the crisis. I hung on so tightly that all I knew was the firmness of my grip. It was an unhappy experience. I was mired in my own concerns. Writing about why it is that Jesus tells the meek they shall be blessed, Simon Tugwell observes:

> If we view life simply in terms of what we can bring about by our own contrivance, we condemn ourselves to a curiously meagre existence. The ultimate goal of everything is God and God cannot be caught by our scheming. To quote Meister

Eckhart, 'Anyone who looks for God in any particular way, gets the way and lets go of God.'[4]

Thinking about outcomes, testing my effort and my resolve, I was always condemned to hope only for the little that I could achieve by myself. I needed to get to the place the judge described. I needed to know it would end well. We read stories one way, when we are in the midst of them, and then understand them very differently when they are over. I needed the happy ending.

'There! Now it is written'

We want our lives to be a story. We would love them to have a happy ending, of course, but we also want them to make sense, to see a kind of pattern. We want our lives to draw to an end with a feeling that something has been finished and completed. Here is Timothy Radcliffe:

> That is why the stories of deathbed repentances are important. The last moment crystallizes all that has gone before. The end of the story sheds a light of meaning on the whole. When the Venerable Bede was dying he had to complete his last writing. 'Then the boy of whom I spoke, whose name is Wilberht, said once again: "There is still one sentence, dear master, that we have not written down". And Bede said, "Write it". After a little the boy said: "There! Now it is written". And Bede replied, "Good! It is finished".'[5]

That is a good story. Confronted with a dying child, however, we really struggle to accept that it could, or should, be *finished*. One of the greatest challenges in ministry is being confronted by a parent (or indeed anyone torn with grief) who asks you to explain what God is doing. 'Why?' they ask. 'What is the point?' Simon Tugwell has written about this and notes how very badly we need a proper ending to the story. Death, he reminds us, robs us of the ending we want. We die, or see others die, and we are left with a brooding sense of all that is unfinished. It is not just the piano left unplayed, or the unfinished bit of needlework on the sofa. It is something much more unsettling. There are sentences that have been left unsaid, questions unanswered, disagreements that were never resolved.

I was invited not so long ago to preach at a school commemoration. It was the end of the school year. The congregation was largely made up of very proud parents and sixth-formers about to launch off to university, or into careers. The staff wore hoods and gowns, there were hats, there were flowers in buttonholes. The air was heavy with achievement. If ever there was a moment for looking back with gratitude and forward with confidence, this was it. Yet oddly, amid the familiar and rather complacent texts, 'Let us now praise famous men . . .', one very different reading stood out. We heard a poem by C. Day Lewis that is apparently read every year. It is called 'Walking Away', and in it, C. Day Lewis describes watching his son trudge back to a school changing room, alone, after a game of football. The boy is new to the school; he is little, and he is lost. He has to find his own way and he struggles to do that, there is 'no path where the path should be'.[6] I am not entirely sure why we heard that poem. It struck a strange and unsettling note amid the confidence of young people hunting down their destiny after A level success. Love, C. Day Lewis tells us, demands a 'letting go'.

Although modern rhetoric affirms ambition, aspiration and living the dream, some of us struggle. Like the small boy in that big school, we worry about the direction of travel more than we like to admit; we find no path where the path should be. R. S. Thomas, in his poem 'Country Clergy', worries that the devotion and hard work of parish clergy (of which he was one) seems so pointless, unfinished, incomplete, crumbling into dust. He looks to God 'in his time, or out of time' to 'correct this'.[7] Tugwell turns instead to Thomas Aquinas who points to *beatitude*: the idea that there is a completion in the hereafter, which is beyond us now, the triumphant and definitive arrival of a human story at its proper and blissful conclusion.[8]

We want to be a story and only with this beatitude can we do that, only here do we get to the proper ending. The point is that only God can provide the ending we miss.

Scripture and the promises of God

This anxiety about the ending is not a modern problem brought on by an excess of zeal for 'demonstrable outcomes'. I think we are cursed with an excessive need for progress, but we have always struggled with our confidence in the future that God secures. The Book of Genesis broods over the nature of God's promises, and trembles over and again on the brink of some calamity that seems to dash down hope. Barren Sarah, Abraham told to take a knife to his son Isaac, Jacob working for Laban but rewarded with Leah and not with Rachel, the twists and turns of the story of Joseph; this is a story that only makes sense as it ends. Think too of the refugees that Moses led out of Egypt, striding between the divided waters of the sea, only to come to a place of doubt and despair.

> The Israelites, the whole congregation, came into the wilderness of Zin in the first month, and the people stayed in Kadesh. Miriam died there, and was buried there. Now there was no water for the congregation; so they gathered together against Moses and against Aaron. The people quarrelled with Moses and said, 'Would that we had died when our kindred died before the LORD! Why have you brought the assembly of the LORD into this wilderness for us and our livestock to die here?' (Numbers 20.1–4)

Scripture wrestles with a story that too often appears to have taken a wrong turning:

The Lord has become like an enemy; he has destroyed Israel. He has destroyed all its palaces, laid in ruins its strongholds, and multiplied in daughter Judah mourning and lamentation. He has broken down his booth like a garden, he has destroyed his tabernacle; the LORD has abolished in Zion festival and sabbath, and in his fierce indignation has spurned king and priest. (Lamentations 2.5–6)

The Gospels remind us starkly that outcomes are not ours to determine. The endings are not ours to confer:

James and John, the sons of Zebedee, came forward to him and said to him, 'Teacher, we want you to do for us whatever we ask of you.' And he said to them, 'What is it you want me to do for you?' And they said to him, 'Grant us to sit, one at your right hand and one at your left, in your glory.' But Jesus said to them, 'You do not know what you are asking. Are you able to drink the cup that I drink, or be baptized with the baptism that I am baptized with?' They replied, 'We are able.' Then Jesus said to them, 'The cup that I drink you will drink; and with the baptism with which I am baptized, you will be baptized; but to sit at my right hand or at my left is not mine to grant, but it is for those for whom it has been prepared.' (Mark 10.35–40)

James and John wanted the ending of the story and they wanted it now. Instead, they got the promise that they would share in the life and suffering of Christ.

It is a fundamental assumption in scripture that we can trust the good purposes of God, but that the beginning and ending of those purposes lie beyond our control or understanding. In Gethsemane, Christ himself wrestled with that fundamentally human dilemma that sees no path where the path should be and struggled to resign his need for purpose and control.

My Father, if it is possible, let this cup pass from me; yet not what I want but what you want. (Matthew 26.39)

There is, interestingly, more than a hint that what Jesus had to resign in the garden of Gethsemane – his grip on his own life, its purpose and meaning – he regained in the final moments on the cross. There, John reminds us, he bowed his head and he gave up (*handed over* might be better) his spirit (John 19.30). Indeed, John insists that Jesus died saying, 'It is finished,' or perhaps, 'It is accomplished.' Jesus died in possession of that certainty, the great work was done. 'It is accomplished.'

Providing an ending

In the chapter on All Souls, I described Michael Mayne's experience facing his own death. He was worried about the pain he might face, but worried just as much about his faith and his ability to surrender a life in which he had so carefully and assiduously conferred *meaning*.

We have to let go. We have to learn to trust in the God who is the storyteller and the beginning and ending that we depend upon. We have to let go, but we find that hard. I have met people who have assured me that they know the ending. They know that they will be reunited with friends and family (and dogs and cats and budgies). I have had people tell me that they will have money in heaven. Life will just go on. In the famous words of Henry Scott Holland, used so often at funerals, 'death is nothing at all, it does not count. I have only slipped away into the next room.'[9] There are people who can trust that.

This kind of language has never seemed very satisfactory to me. My encounters with death, when friends or relatives have died, have always reminded me that death is sharp and sudden and utterly dislocating. Interestingly, that is exactly what Holland thought. That famous passage, so often quoted, comes from a sermon preached at St Paul's Cathedral after the death of Edward VII. Holland pulls the rug from under our feet. There are different ways of looking at death, he argued. You could say that 'Death is nothing at all'. Or, instead, you could suggest that death is the supreme and irrevocable disaster. It is the impossible, the incredible thing. Nothing leads up to it, nothing prepares for it. It simply traverses every line on which life runs, cutting across every hope on which life feeds, and every intention which gives life significance. It makes all we do here mean-ingless and empty.[10]

Holland argues that we live between knowing nothing and knowing everything. He can reassure us that we know that we are children of God and there is a future. Yet, we cannot describe that future:

We can see nothing ahead. No hint reaches us to interpret it. How can we picture it? How can we give it concrete and actual expression? We gaze and gaze, and the abyss is blind and black. Death shuts fast the door. Beyond the darkness hides its impenetrable secret.[11]

He is a lot less reassuring than he is usually made to sound. He quotes the First Epistle of John to remind us that 'We know not now what we shall be'. There is an ending, but it is out of our hands.

So, scripture and experience tell me that we will encounter loss and we will struggle. We will find it hard to name the future we long for. When we come to that place, it is the creed that provides the language for the hope we seek. It is the creed that gives us the words: 'the forgiveness of sins, the resurrec-tion of the body, and the life everlasting'. It is doctrine, the teaching of the Church, that offers us the ending that we seek.

We will see no angels

Before I was ordained priest, I studied and then taught his-tory. The man who supervised my research was called Eamon Duffy (whose writing has been quoted here a number of times). He is a scholar of reformation, a theologian and a practising

Catholic. As his name rather implies, he is also Irish. After I was ordained I became chaplain of the college in which Eamon works (and before you raise a suspicious eyebrow, he was not on the appointment panel). Fellows of the same college, I would occasionally invite him to preach to us in the college chapel. Some of those sermons preached in Magdalene (with others delivered elsewhere) are now published in a collection called *Walking to Emmaus*. The sermon that gives the collection its title was preached in Westminster Abbey. It is all about finding meaning; making a journey 'into meaning'. Duffy begins with memories of Easter Sunday marches to a cemetery that were a fixture in his childhood:

> Like hundreds of other people I was following a dozen grey haired men carrying rifles, marching to a brass band behind drums and banners. Often they were led by my father, as officer in charge of the flag party. At the graveyard the procession made its way to the Republican plot with its granite monument to those who had fallen in the fight for Irish Freedom. There those veterans of the Irish war of Independence and the Irish Civil war raised their rifles and fired a volley of shots over the grave.[12]

He goes on to talk about a childhood steeped in the story of Ireland's 1916 Easter Rising. As he learnt it, this was a story of suffering and loss, but also of renewal and *rising*. His procession to the graveyard reprised that story and gave him a place within it,

> so that Easter afternoon walk, towards our dead, really did seem a walk into meaning.[13]

He is describing powerful memories, but he fixes them under the sort of lens that a historian should apply. Duffy knows that the stories we tell can and do inspire, but they can also badly mislead us. He talks about 'terrible self-delusion' and our ability to construct a meaning that suits us, creating a story of our own. On that platform, he then builds his sermon about the Emmaus road. He explains how Jesus opens up the past and explains it to the two disciples walking away from Jerusalem.

> He leads them through the whole of the Jewish Scriptures, to show how his life and suffering and death really do make sense, that if only they could see it properly, this was the fulfilment they and all God's people had been waiting for.[14]

This, Duffy argues, is the story we can trust. This is the story we need to hear, and hearing it we should then join in. Christ invites us to walk with him 'into meaning':

> Not to a place of tombs, not to seek the living among the dead, but to hear again his words, to walk with him on his way. There, however uncertain we are, however weak our faith, or faltering our hope, we find food for the journey and companionship along the way. There our hearts can respond to his word, to the promises of his kingdom which he will bring, and which we can work for. We will see no angels, there will be no flags, or trumpets, but we have no need of them. The Lord is near, he is in the midst of us, he is known to us in the breaking of the bread.[15]

As the sermon builds to a climax, it sweeps us along. Duffy does not underestimate the difficulty, however, and neither should we. He reminds us that the disciples on the road were 'bewildered' and that like them we might not recognize the Christ who comes to us. We might feel 'uncertain'; he is clear that there will be no flags, no trumpets, and that we will see no angels. There *is* a story; we can hear it and we can be part of it, but it never was easy reassurance. It is a good story, it is a true story and it offers an ending we had not thought of. But it is a story we have to learn and to trust.

Faith is a form of trust. To believe in God is to trust that the lives we live so intensely and so briefly have a beginning and ending we cannot see. Easy to say, hard to put into practice.

The business of living in trust has always been a challenge. The disciples who set out with Jesus so eagerly always struggled to 'follow' him. The Gospels (particularly Mark) record their confusions:

> A great gale arose . . . they woke him up and said to him, 'Teacher, do you not care that we are perishing?' He woke up and rebuked the wind . . . He said to them, 'Why are you afraid? Have you still no faith?' (Mark 4.37–40)

> His disciples [said], 'How can one feed these people with bread here in the desert?' (Mark 8.4)

> But turning and looking at his disciples, he rebuked Peter and said, 'Get behind me, Satan! For you are setting your mind not on divine things but on human things.' (Mark 8.33)

> And the disciples were perplexed at these words. But Jesus said to them again, 'Children, how hard it is to enter the kingdom of God!' (Mark 10.24)

> A certain young man was following him, wearing nothing but a linen cloth. They caught hold of him, but he left the linen cloth and ran off naked. (Mark 14.51–52)

A boisterous poem by U. A. Fanthorpe called 'Getting It Across' nails the sheer difficulty of teaching the Disciples, with their 'yokel faces', to trust. They just cannot. 'The vital mnemonics they never remember.'[16]

Living within a longer story

Faith might appear to us to be a personal thing, a matter of choice, a point of freedom. That is certainly the way we often talk about faith. Of course, there are moments of conversion, and times when God seems close at hand. What scripture says, though, is that faith is a lesson learnt slowly and not without difficulty. Faith is the life to which we are summoned, and at first it really does not come naturally. It is always on the road following Jesus. That is why we have a creed and that is why we need doctrine. Here the experience we have not had, the life we have yet to live and the ending we do not know are put into the words we need to learn. Say the word 'doctrine' and you conjure up images of dusty dons and heavy tomes. Worse, there is a hint of something oppressive and life-denying: 'He is doctrinaire', 'She is indoctrinated'. Doctrine, though, is just teaching. The Latin root is *docere*, 'to teach', and it gives us *doctrine* and the *doctors* who can teach. We have creeds and sermons and a year of grace to help us learn and live the lessons. Faith is always the gift of God, but we have to learn how to live it.

Faith sets our lives within a narrative that stretches on and on. At times of stress and suffering that can be very hard to bear. We cannot understand and we can find no reassurance. Our hope has to depend on things we cannot see and cannot control. We are back where we were at All Souls, looking for answers we cannot name, back with C. S. Lewis and 'news from a country we have never yet visited'. Writing to the bereaved, over the years, I have sometimes turned to a poem, 'Autumn' by Rainer Maria Rilke:

> The leaves are falling, falling as from far,
> as though above were withering farthest gardens;
> they fall with a denying attitude.
> And night by night, down into solitude,
> the heavy earth falls far from every star.
> We are all falling. This hand's falling too –
> all have this falling-sickness none withstands.
> And yet there's One whose gently-holding hands
> this universal falling can't fall through.[17]

It is in the teaching of the Church, in its doctrine, that this confidence is set forth.

Notes

1 H. McCabe, *Law, Language and Love* (London: Bloomsbury Continuum, 2004), pp. 128–9.

2 N. Lash, *Believing Three Ways in One God* (Norwich: SCM Press, 2010), p. 31.

3 C. S. Lewis, *The Screwtape Letters* (London: William Collins, 2016), p. 16.

4 S. Tugwell, *The Beatitudes: Soundings in Christian Tradition* (Springfield, IL: Templegate, 1980), pp. 36–7.

5 T. Radcliffe, *What is the Point of Being a Christian?* (London: Burns and Oates, 2005), p. 87.

6 C. Day Lewis, 'Walking Away' in *The Gate and Other Poems* (London: Jonathan Cape, 1962).

7 R. S. Thomas, 'County Clergy' in *Collected Poems* (London: J. M. Dent, 1993), p. 82.

8 S. Tugwell, *Human Immortality and the Redemption of Death* (London: Darton, Longman & Todd, 1990), p. 154.

9 Henry Scott Holland, 'Death the King of Terrors', 1910, available at https://en.wikisource.org/wiki/The_King_of_Terrors (accessed 21 May 2019).

10 Holland, 'Death the King of Terrors'.

11 Holland, 'Death the King of Terrors'.

12 E. Duffy, *Walking to Emmaus* (London: Burns and Oates, 2006), p. 79.

13 Duffy, *Walking to Emmaus*, p. 80.

14 Duffy, *Walking to Emmaus*, pp. 83–4.

15 Duffy, *Walking to Emmaus*, p. 85.

16 U. A. Fanthorpe, 'Getting It Across' in *New and Collected Poems* (London: Enitharmon Press, 2010).

17 R. M. Rilke, 'Autumn' in *Selected Poems* (London: Penguin, 1972), p. 25.

20

A Year of Belief

I am trying to persuade you (in case you need persuading) that doctrine matters and doctrine helps. I have tried to show how we bump into doctrine throughout the year. I have explained a little how that liturgical year and doctrine have helped me. You will know by now that I believe that we all need saving from ourselves. Doctrine does that.

In the course of the Church's year, something is happening *around* us, something we do not control, and something is happening *to* us. However much we would like to think that the liturgical year is something we have made and which we keep (in the way that we talk about *keeping* Christmas), the truth is that it is the year that takes charge. Eamon Duffy spoke of a journey into meaning. Our year of grace is a journey into truth. It teaches us what we might become. Learning that lesson, though, requires a commitment from us.

'I don't think doctrine is my thing'

I have already explained that doctrine is just teaching. Theology is simply the Church's way of talking about God (as theologians keep reminding us, the word *theology* means nothing more threatening than 'God talk'). So, it is unfortunate that the Church has managed to make something that ought to be fundamental – talking about God – into an academic pastime conducted behind closed faculty doors. There is an awful lot of theology out there. I have spent a lot of my life reading it and talking about it. Even so, I still find some of it hard to understand and I know that theology seldom seems to prove its relevance.

Years ago, training to be a priest at a college just outside Oxford, I started a course in doctrine. I had already studied a bit of doctrine at university, though if I am honest I had not really enjoyed that very much. I thought of myself more as a historian (interested in stories, you see) and this was just a necessary hurdle to jump. Starting this new course, I imagined that I would be able to knock off a few essays and then move on. Because I had studied some doctrine before, it was decided that I would not do the college course aimed at beginners. I was sent down the road to the university for tutorials by myself. That seemed fine in principle, but the first essay turned out to be a bit of a nightmare. The work I had done in the past had always been a study of just one theologian. I had been asked, 'What did Augustine have to say about sin?' or 'Why did Aquinas think theology was important?' Some of the books were dense and occasionally I had to lie down between sentences, but all you really had to do was make a kind of list and you had an answer. Now, in Oxford, the rules changed. I was asked what I believed and why. I struggled and went to the tutorial a bit downcast and hoping to muddle through. My tutor had made me some tea. Thinking it wise to get in first, I suggested to him that he should not expect too much. 'I don't think doctrine is my thing,' I said. He slapped the table, spilling the tea. 'If you are going to be a parish priest,' he said, 'doctrine had bloody well better be your thing.'

The next essay was rather better. At first I worked at it because doctrine really mattered to him. Then doctrine began to matter to me. Twenty years later, it was me doing the teaching. I was with a group of curates and we had spent half a day or so talking about what God might be like and in particular about whether or not God *suffers*. As our day drew to a close, one of the curates had had more than enough and told me, 'I don't think this is my bag; I think this is much more your sort of thing than mine.' I did not knock over any drinks, but I think I replied, pretty robustly, something about doctrine being very definitely your 'bag' if you were a parish priest.

Doctrine matters. Let's take the example that upset that curate, the question of whether or not God suffers. We know that the Son of God suffers on the cross. We know that suffering is very heart of what it meant for Jesus to take flesh.

Was it not necessary that the Messiah should suffer these things and then enter into his glory? (Luke 24.26)

The trouble is, that leaves a question begging. Why does there have to be all this suffering? Our own suffering, our pain, our fear and grief, all that we know about disease and death, demands an explanation. It is one thing to say that Christ shares it. It is quite another to ask, why is all this agony necessary? Why does a good God allow this? Theologians have always asked those questions and they have offered us various answers. In the last 75 years or so, the debate has shifted. Our horror has been getting better informed. Thanks to television and technology, horror has been made more horrible and more visible. In the gas chambers of the Holocaust, in the slaughterhouses of the Khmer Rouge, and in countless places besides, we have demonstrated that we can kill on an industrial scale. The questions have got sharper and more insistent. As that has happened, theology has adapted. Once we took it as a kind of rule that God is *impassible*. We argued that God does not have feelings and does not react with pain, or pleasure, as events unfold. Now you will find more and more theologians arguing that this cannot be true. They want to reassure us that God the Father is not unmoved by our terrible agony, not remote, not indifferent. The only way they can make sense of all this pain is to tell us that God shares it too. Plenty of theologians are now prepared to say that not only does Jesus suffer on the cross but God the Father suffers too. It is an idea not confined to thick books on library shelves. You will find it in our hymns. W. H. Vanstone's 'Morning glory, starlit sky' urges us to accept that God is *drained* in the act of creation:

Here is God: no monarch he,
throned in easy state to reign;
here is God, whose arms of love
aching, spent, the world sustain.[1]

Similarly, Timothy Rees' hymn 'God is Love: let heaven adore
Him' tells us:

And when human hearts are breaking
under sorrow's iron rod,
then they find that selfsame aching
deep within the heart of God.

This is doctrine and it is shifting. Our theology has changed.
Big books enter the debate and we are not going to settle it
here. You can argue that in the Old Testament we meet a God
who can be indignant, furious, jealous, and then suddenly merciful and generous. You can argue that the old philosophical
categories we have used to describe God are dated and need to
be refreshed. You can argue that God is not like anything else
and does not have to conform to what our logic requires. Bits
of that argument can get very technical. Even so, you should
not say that this is just an *academic* argument and that it does
not matter. A God who suffers, a God who feels pain, may
well be more appealing (and more human) than a God who
is remote and impassible. The trouble is, a God who suffers is
just another victim, and as Vanstone's hymn puts it, this God
is 'weak' and 'helpless'. If you believe that, you have solved one
problem (the problem of a God who creates a world of pain
and then seems indifferent to our agony) and you have created
another. Now you need to explain how this weak and helpless
God can save us. You need to explain how a God that can be
hurt by creation is the God who is Lord of that creation. If
there are things out there that can hurt God, is God really God
of all that is? The answers to these questions matter fundamentally. If we have no answer, our salvation hangs on a breaking

thread. It matters. Doctrine gives, or does not give, the words of life.

Meeting the saints

Doctrine matters and doctrine helps. I irritated my tutor in doctrine because my interests were elsewhere. I first studied theology because it was the best option for someone who liked church history. I did as much church history as I could, and got very interested indeed in the Reformation. It was as a historian, researching the late sixteenth and early seventeenth centuries, that I was taught by Eamon Duffy. While I was scratching away at a thesis, he was writing something much more significant. His book *The Stripping of the Altars* gave us a new way of looking at the Reformation. He wrote about churches and what was in them. He set out to tell us (because we rather doubted it) that there was plenty of evidence that traditional, Catholic faith was very much alive and well when Henry VIII set us against Rome.

If you pick up *The Stripping of the Altars*, you will find pictures of fonts, bench ends and painted saints. Duffy describes the way people prayed and discusses their ideas about death. There were days when he drove to Norfolk to look at churches and take pictures. Because looking at churches was altogether more to my taste than yet another day with the manuscripts in the library, I sometimes went with him.

It was on those jaunts that I began to see that theology can and should break out of the classroom. I met the saints and discovered that they had a point to make. We used to go and look at rood screens in those Norfolk churches. A rood screen is, essentially, a wooden partition in a church, solid up to chest height but then sprouting graceful arches, making windows. These screens separated the choir of the church from the nave. There were gates in the centre of the screen, so that you could get up to the high altar at the Mass. High up above those arches and 'windows' was a great beam on which there would have been a crucifix, with statues of the Blessed Virgin Mary and St John on either side. If you had stepped into the church in the fifteenth or early sixteenth centuries, this great cross would have stopped you in your tracks. It was this that gave the screen its name, *rood* being a medieval name for the cross. There was the death of Christ, right at the heart of the community. If you were in church for a Mass you would have knelt under the cross. You would have been reminded, very physically, of your place in the story of salvation. As you knelt, you would also have been keeping some startling company, because the panelling was painted with images of saints. You would have knelt next to the Apostles, perhaps, or a company of martyrs.

These saints had purpose and attitude. At a very simple level, kneeling next to St Peter, St Andrew and St James, week by week at Mass, the faithful in villages like Ranworth or Worstead got a visible reminder that they really did worship in the same church as the Apostles. Their religion never could be merely local; holiness never could be just a way of trying to be good today and tomorrow. The faithful knew that they were part of a Church that *shared* the faith across the ages, across a world. Occasionally, one of the saints on the rood was a local figure like St Walstan of Bawburgh, a vivid celebration of the fact that sanctity is possible in places like this.

These were images that told the faithful something about the nature of the Church. They set believers in a greater company and made them look around. At Ranworth, which has one of the most staggeringly beautiful of all these rood screens, there was a very particular lesson to be learnt. There you can see the Apostles ranked and rallied across the centre of the church. Look to your right, however, and there is something else. There, the screen blocks off an aisle and there is an altar. Above the altar are more saints, the three Marys – the Blessed Virgin, Mary Salome and Mary Cleophas – and with them St Margaret. They are there for a reason. Margaret was the patron saint of childbirth; the three Marys appear with their children and their children's toys. A child blows bubbles, another has a little windmill. Here was an altar where the women of

Ranworth went to pray for safe delivery, or for their children, or indeed to pray if they wished for children. Here was another reminder that local concerns, the familiar worries about children, were part of a much bigger story. They had their place in what we say about lives that are created and redeemed.

This is doctrine made visible. The Apostles, sometimes carrying scrolls of text spelling out the creed, were there to teach. Routinely these apostles would appear in two rows of six on the left and right sides of the screen. That left the four central panels, on the two doors that gave access to the high altar. Often painted on those doors you would see images of St Jerome, St Gregory, St Ambrose and St Augustine, the 'four Latin doctors', the recognized symbols of the Church's teaching. To receive communion, you had to pass through the teaching of the Church: you got there via doctrine.

This was a church that was so much more at ease with theology or doctrine then we are now. This was a church that was eager to talk about God because it was determined that we should not be always talking about ourselves. The women who came to Ranworth came with overwhelming hopes and fears. They lived close to sudden death and feared illnesses they could not name. Their anxiety for their children and their own uncertainty brought them to the little altar in the south aisle, and there in the company of saints their concerns were all gathered in. A bustling, modern earnestness turns its back on that Ranworth altar. It thinks that those women were credulous, and suspects that they prayed to the saints in the hope of some magic that might put things right. It assumes that their faith was desperate and vague. The truth is different. The people of Ranworth did not pray to the saints looking for favours. They lived and prayed with the saints. That was what faith and theology told them, that they belonged in a Church. They kept company with saints. Their fears and hopes did not just matter to them, they mattered always in a community stretched out over time and space. Their story, the story of women with children, the very domestic story of our concern for our own children, was a story they could read in scripture and see in church. That is what theology can do. It can talk about God when you are tempted just to talk about yourself. The theology of the Ranworth screen refused to leave a village alone with its faith. It spoke of God; it put them in the company of saints. It gave everyone a glimpse of the faith of the whole Church.

A bigger picture

Doctrine reminds us to talk about God. Doctrine reminds us that fascinating as we undoubtedly are, we are only part of a story that sweeps up the women of Ranworth, the saints, prophets and patriarchs and creation itself. The creed, spelt out in the Christian year, gathers us into a story of grace and gives us a beginning and an ending that otherwise escape us. The creed and the liturgical year do not just inform and teach us. They persuade us to look up and look around, to notice the scale and sweep of the story we should tell. We do have to be prepared to learn a little. We do have to make a commitment. The alternative is to be left talking to ourselves, about ourselves.

Believing in the Church

It is not just that we are saved from ourselves. One of the reasons we need the doctrine of the creed and the rhythm of the Christian year is because it will throw back the curtains and make us admire the view. We tell the whole story; we find our part in something greater than ourselves. Margaret Drabble once wonderfully described the significance of reading the Bible:

> the Bible was different. It was grand, extreme and horrid. It spoke damnation and darkness, it sounded cymbals and trumpets, it flared its nostrils and it sniffed another air. Deserts and mountains, valleys and springs, pits and entombments, cedars of Lebanon and rose of Sharon, fishpools of Heshbon and vineyards of Samaria.[2]

Faith should do that for us, set us in a bigger room. A prayer of Hilary of Poitiers is a plea for this breadth of vision: 'Almighty God, bestow on me the meaning of words, the light of understanding, nobility of diction and faith in the truth.'[3] It is the whole story we need.

Theology is the *whole* story. Theology is also *our* story.

Years ago, I spent an evening with Michael Mayne (the man who had been my vicar once). I asked him if he was writing. He was, he told me, writing a book of letters to his grandchildren. I don't think I pulled a face, but I felt as though I was pulling a face. The letters apparently were all about *wonder*. I thought it all sounded a touch twee and I changed the subject. I should have known better. Mayne's book *This Sunrise of Wonder* is now something of a classic and a book I return to over and again. It is both a theological meditation on wonder and an anthology of quotation from a literary life. He knew that faith needs a dash of astonishment. He was well aware of the limits of what he knew.

He noted that

Isaac Bashevis Singer, the Jewish novelist, used a good metaphor for where we stand in relation to God: It is as if you were to ask a book-worm crawling inside a copy of *War and Peace* whether it is a good novel or a bad one. He is sitting on one letter trying to get a little nourishment. How can he be a critic of Tolstoy?[4]

How can I know God? I cannot. I simply cannot comprehend that holiness, that life so different from my own. I can, however, know Christ and I can live the story of the Christian year. I can find my place in the story.

Michael Mayne's ashes are now interred in Westminster Abbey where he was dean. There is a quotation from Boethius on the memorial stone:

Thou art the journey and the journey's end.

To come to God (which we cannot do by navigation, only by grace) we need to make that journey. It is an annual event. It is the year of grace.

Notes

1 W. H. Vanstone, 'Morning glory, starlit sky'. Reproduced by permission.

2 M. Drabble, *The Peppered Moth* (QPD, 2000), pp. 8–9.

3 G. Appleton (ed.), *The Oxford Book of Prayer* (Oxford: Oxford University Press, 1985), p. 119.

4 M. Mayne, *This Sunrise of Wonder: Letters for the Journey* (London: Fount, 1995), p. 58.

Acknowledgements of Sources

E. Jennings, 'The Annunciation', *Collected Poems* (London: Carcanet Press, 1986, p. 45), David Higham Associates.

L. MacNeice, 'Snow', *Collected Poems* (London: Faber, 1966), p. 30, David Higham Associates.

J. R. Peacey, 'For Mary, Mother of the Lord', *Revised English Hymnal* (Norwich: Hymns Ancient and Modern, forthcoming 2019), M. J. Hancock. Permission applied for.

D. Sayers, 'The Just Vengeance' [1946] quoted in *Believing in the Church: The Corporate Nature of Faith* (London: SPCK, 1981), p. 1, David Higham Associates.

D. Sayers, *The Man Born to be King* (London: Gollancz, 1943), first broadcast on 21 December 1941, David Higham Associates.

W. H. Vanstone, 'Morning glory, starlit sky', *Revised English Hymnal* (Norwich: Hymns Ancient and Modern, forthcoming 2019) © W. H. Vanstone 1923–1999, J. W. Shore, reproduced by permission.